LEANING
into
LOVE

a spiritual journey
through grief

ELAINE MANSFIELD

Larson Publications
Burdett, New York

ISBN-10: 1-936012-72-3
ISBN-13: 978-1-936012-72-5
eISBN-10: 1-936012-73-1
eISBN-13: 978-1-936012-73-2

Back cover photo: Susan Kahn / Colgate University
Front cover photo: Vic Mansfield 2007

Library of Congress Control Number: 2014944219

Publisher's Cataloging-In-Publication Data
(Prepared by The Donohue Group, Inc.)

Mansfield, Elaine.
   Leaning into love : a spiritual journey through grief / Elaine Mansfield.

   pages ; cm

   Issued also as an ebook.
   ISBN-13: 978-1-936012-72-5
   ISBN-10: 1-936012-72-3

   1. Mansfield, Elaine--Family. 2. Grief--Psychological aspects. 3. Husbands--Death--Psychological aspects. 4. Love. 5. Widows--United States--Psychology.
I. Title.

BF575.G7 M36 2014
155.9/37092   2014944219

Published by Larson Publications
4936 State Route 414
Burdett, New York 14818 USA

http://larsonpublications.com

23 22 21 3019 18 17 16 15 14
10 9 8 7 6 5 4 3 2 1

LEANING
into
LOVE

For Vic—
my lover, husband, spiritual partner,
and best friend.

People do not
pass away.

They die,
and then

they stay.

−*Naomi Shihab Nye*
(with permission of the author)

Contents

Oceans

I have a feeling that my boat
has struck, down there in the depths,
against a great thing.

And nothing
happens! Nothing . . . Silence . . . Waves. . . .

—Nothing happens? Or has everything happened,
and are we standing now, quietly, in the new life?[1]

1

Gone Beyond.
Oh, What an Awakening.

"He's conscious," the nurse says. I trust this
Vietnam vet with his acne scarred face and tender resigned heart. His
sad eyes help me face what's coming. The two of us stand next to a bed
in the oncology unit of Strong Hospital and look over Vic's limp body.

"He can hear you," the nurse says, "but he's too exhausted to respond.
You can ask him to squeeze your hand."

Yes, I could ask Vic to squeeze my hand if he loves me. But I don't
doubt his love. I can ask him to squeeze if he hears me, but he doesn't
need to hear me. He needs to die, so I don't call him back to life and to
me, but let him stay with the hard labor of breathing. I touch him and
inhale his scent, rub oil into his hands and feet, and pray for strength to
let him go. I've walked with him to the threshold of death and hung my
feet over the ledge. I feel the vastness of the abyss, but can go no further.

For two years I've tried to save him. We've both tried, but there are
no more escape routes. After years of struggle, his gentle passage opens
my heart and stills my mind. This quiet death is his last gift to me, even
as I weep and whisper my good-byes. Just after midnight, he exhales. I
wait for an inhalation that does not come.

I don't know how to live without this man. I depend on his brown eyes beaming at me. For forty-two years we loved each other, meditated together, transformed our land, raised our sons, and shared our dreams and sorrows. I don't know who I am without him.

I sit with his body for six hours, until an orderly takes him away in a body bag. Then I walk down the dark hospital corridor toward the elevator, my shoulder leaning into my son Anthony. We're followed by four friends who stayed with Vic and me at the hospital the last three days. I'm exhausted and numb, but also relieved. I don't have to watch his suffering anymore. Now I begin to deal with my own.

We take the elevator down and walk toward the hospital lobby, shading our eyes from the sun glaring through the floor-to-ceiling windows. People scurry, grasping coffee cups, pushing to punch in before seven a.m. They are serious and self-absorbed, their eyes averted. They are behind a glass wall, in another world, on the side of the living. I stand on a threshold where death feels closer than life.

We find my Subaru in the parking garage and stack Vic's clothes and laptop on the back seat. Lingering, we stand in a helpless clump, softened by the mystery of death we just witnessed. It's not enough to hug and thank these generous friends for accompanying me on this journey, but it's all I have to give.

"Are you OK to drive?" Anthony asks.

"Yes," I answer. "Follow me."

I steer down the parking garage ramp, driving slowly so Anthony can catch up in his rental car. I stop at the parking attendant's glass-windowed booth. My body knows how to count the money and pay the parking fee. *Isn't there a discount if the person you brought here has been left behind in the morgue?* It's a ghoulish private joke the young parking lot attendant won't get. I'm a stranger, just returned from the underworld. I've seen death, raw and unstoppable, and understand that my own death is not a distant thing.

My body knows how to navigate this world, knows the way to the airport where Anthony can return his car. I grip the steering wheel, feeling both sharply awake and vaguely disembodied. Outside the rental car return, I move into the passenger seat and let the June sun bathe me with warmth.

Anthony drives toward home in the slow lane on the New York State Thruway. We travel over the foreign soil of this world, strangers to the usual concerns of the day.

"Are you OK?" Lauren asks when she calls the next morning. Lauren Cottrell is one of the friends who attended Vic's death. She helped me swab his mouth, hold his body, chant prayers, and read passages out loud from *The Tibetan Book of Living and Dying.*

"Nothing is solid. It's all a dream," I tell her. "The mortician said that if I want to put anything in Vic's cremation box, it should happen today before his body begins to decompose. It feels important to do this right, but I'm floating and spinning."

"I'm on my way," Lauren says. "I'll sit quietly or help however I can."

I stand at the bathroom sink and inspect the drawn woman in the mirror with dark circles under her eyes. Her gray hair falls in limp clumps and her red eyes are puffy, but nothing remarkable has changed on the outside. I still have a body and it needs a shower. The hot water pounds my tight neck. It feels good, just like it did when I took a shower in Vic's hospital room a few days ago. I'm grateful for the small pleasure. I gel and brush my hair for the first time in days, put on tan workout pants, my favorite apricot tank top, and slip my bare feet into Birkenstocks. I glance in the mirror again. *How am I supposed to do this?* Not expecting a response, I go downstairs, make myself a bowl of yogurt, and brew a cup of mint tea to settle my stomach.

My older son David joins me on the back porch. He arrived late last night. Purple shadows under his brown eyes tell of yesterday's long sad journey from the mountains of Slovakia. He knew he wouldn't get home in time to see his dad alive.

The warm morning light helps me find my bearings. Finches jockey for perches at the bird feeder. Red-winged blackbirds and blue jays complain. I sit at the picnic table inhaling the steam of my mint tea, trying to focus my racing mind on the list of tasks. Do I want to pay for an obituary in Vic's hometown newspaper, even though he hasn't lived there for fifty years? Should the memorial service be Sunday afternoon or next month? How do I plan a memorial service anyway? What do I do about the flower arrangements with their cloying smells and pastel colors? They are delivered one after another, and my house reeks.

Lauren walks around the side of the house toward the porch, moving with a bounce even though she hasn't slept for days either. She hugs David's sturdy weightlifter's body and sits next to me, wrapping an arm around my waist. Her long brown hair is damp and smells faintly of shampoo. I hear Anthony grinding coffee in the kitchen and catch a whiff of French roast. He joins us on the back porch, his eyes just as red and swollen as David's and mine.

"What's happening, Mom?" he asks. "How can I help?"

"We need to figure out what to put in your dad's cremation box."

David and Lauren help me pack a basket with Vic's favorite foods, books, poems, and flowers while Anthony prints photographs. Yesterday afternoon, Anthony and I bought a swaddling cloth for Vic. I ran my fingers over every white blanket in Kmart on Route 13 in Ithaca and chose the softest one. Vic liked a soft cover.

As we leave the house, I grab two hawk feathers I found on our land and tuck them inside the basket.

Early this morning, the funeral home transported Vic's body from the hospital in Rochester to Ithaca for cremation. I have to identify him. I'm glad I'll see his body one last time.

Vic's mom Virginia is too devastated to see her only child's body, so we drop Anthony at her apartment in Ithaca on the way to the funeral home. I don't want her to be alone. Virginia is a strong ninety-two-year-old, but she hasn't seen Vic much the last few months.

"God won't do this to me," she told me when I encouraged her to takes the rides I arranged to our home or the hospital. She was wrong and now she carries the extra burden of not saying good-bye.

The mortician greets us in a hushed voice and guides us through darkened rooms. His studied seriousness and the smell of this place remind me all too much of the flurry of florist deliveries. As we enter the room where Vic's body is stored, a mouse scoots across the cement floor. The funeral director grabs a broom and chases the mouse under a cabinet. Lauren, David, and I giggle, assuring him that we country folk are used to rodents, but he blushes and stammers apologies. Vic would love the comic relief.

Even though I gave orders not to do anything artificial to his body, Vic looks better dead than he looked alive during the last month. His body lies on a stainless steel table, his face relaxed, youthful, and handsome. I thought I might recoil, but instead my heart opens toward his sweet abandoned body.

David and I line the cardboard cremation box with the white blanket. The mortician raises Vic with a lift while David holds his dad's feet and I hold his head in my hands. Lauren stands back and watches. I float dreamlike, watching my tears dampen Vic's dark, close-cropped hair as we guide him into the box. I've wept so many tears for Vic. It's good a few of them will burn with him.

I watch my hands touch Vic's cold body from a great distance and wonder if I'm in shock or if my calm is the fruit of years of meditation. Lauren stands close to me while David and I cover Vic's chest and legs with the rectangle of maroon and gold Indian silk that covered him in the hospital. Over his heart, I put a photo of our spiritual teacher Anthony Damiani, a handful of dried flowers saved from a meeting with the Dalai Lama, a red rose, and a purple iris. We make a pillow of the three books Vic wrote.

"He may need his precious ideas wherever he's going," I say, half serious, half teasing.

David props large photos along the inside walls of the box so that

Vic's body lies within a mural of what he loved—his family, teachers, and students. Then he puts a photo of the Dalai Lama hugging Vic close to Vic's face, the same picture we kept at his bedside for the last six weeks. The last photo is of Virginia and Vic from 1963. She wears a cone-shaped feathered turquoise hat and a mink stole with delicate furry paws hanging over her shoulders.

I glance over at the mortician, but he discreetly avoids my gaze. I uncurl Vic's left hand and put a bar of bittersweet chocolate with almonds in it to wish Vic sweetness in the next life. In his right hand, I place a small pomegranate-shaped vase made by my friend Barbara. I filled the vase with coffee beans this morning with a prayer for a conscious afterlife journey. We tuck a box of rigatoni next to Vic's shoulder, in case he craves his favorite pasta in the underworld.

David puts a jaunty hawk feather behind each of his dad's ears. We pause to admire our work, then gather the edges of the white blanket and swaddle Vic's body and all that accompanies him into a tidy wrap. I caress his face one last time before covering it and closing the cardboard lid. As a last blessing, Lauren writes the Buddhist mantra *Om Mani Padme Hum*—Hail to the jewel in the lotus of the heart—in Sanskrit on the outside of the box, just over the crown of Vic's head.

There is nothing more to do.

I turn away from death and face the rest of my life.

◈ ◈

"We're going out for a while, Mom. We won't be late," Anthony tells me that evening.

"Is that OK?" David asks.

"I don't mind at all," I say. Anthony and David are in their thirties and were close to their dad. I'm glad they'll get a chance to talk without me around.

Alone for the first time in days, I climb the stairs and lie on my bed. The first floor of the house feels vacant without Vic, but I'm used to being alone upstairs. In his last months, he was too weak to climb the stairs. Lying in twilight, I remember the piece of silk Sankaracharya gave me in India and long to touch it. I find it in the same drawer where I found Vic's silk a few days ago. Mine is cardinal red with gold threads.

What do we do with these? I had wondered when Sankaracharya's attendants passed us two 4 × 7 foot pieces of silk cloth in 1993. Sri Sankara was the head of South Indian Hinduism in a lineage that began in 788 AD. Pilgrims and prime ministers, travelers and local devotees came to his temple in Kanchipuram to receive his blessing. Surrounded by the wealthy trappings of the temple and his position, Sankara had few possessions other than his staff, sandals, and the long saffron colored cotton wrap of a *saddhu* or renunciate. He was ancient, nearly a hundred years old, and frail with one milky eye blinded by a cataract and the other calmly watching the crowds in front of him. He spent his days with his attendants in a modest concrete-floored open space where devotees visited.

Vic and I had traveled to India for our second visit hoping for the inner stillness of a meditation retreat. The clamor of pleading supplicants, trumpeting of temple elephants, and noisy mayhem surrounding the sage shocked us even though we'd been there before. Despite the outer chaos, my mind became remarkably still in Sankara's presence.

Each morning on the way to the temple, I stopped at the stall of a barefoot woman who sat by the road stringing small pastel and white jasmine flowers into garlands. With her help, I chose the freshest strands to offer to the sage. Besides flowers, devotees brought dried fruit, sweets, jewels, and the silks that made Kanchipuram famous. Sankara blessed what people brought and passed the gifts on to other devotees.

One morning, Sankara held a small stack of colorful silk close to his heart and then his forehead before whispering in his male attendant's ear and pointing toward us and a few other Americans. The attendant handed each of us a folded piece of silk: maroon for Vic, red for me. We felt undeserving, but thrilled. Vic and I brought the silks home and I stored them in an empty dresser drawer with dried rose petals from the Dalai Lama, Buddhist *malas*, and Hindu prayer beads.

Four days ago, when I understood that Vic's death was close, I retrieved his maroon silk and took it to the hospital to cover him.

Sitting on my bed tonight, I wrap my silk around my shoulders and feel the silent comfort of Sankara's blessing. Tomorrow, I'll tell David and Anthony to put this cloth over my body when I die. For now, the silk is my cocoon.

∽ ∾

Two days later, David and Anthony drive me to the crematorium near Ithaca on another exuberant June morning. A cluster of friends waits for us outside. David and Anthony stand close to me as morticians slide Vic's cremation box into the oven.

"Do you want to light the fire, Mrs. Mansfield?" a man's voice asks from behind me.

I step forward to my assigned place before the oven door. The man points to a red button and instructs me to push firmly. I push. Nothing happens. Is this a dream?

"The fire warms for half an hour and then ignites the chamber," the voice behind me explains. I peer through a narrow window in the oven door and spot the edge of Vic's cardboard box. I want to throw my body against the door and wail.

Instead, I exhale, turn, and walk away with David and Anthony. *Om Mani Padme Hum.*

A mortician shows us into a formal parlor in the funeral home next door. We read passages about the after-death experience from *The Tibetan Book of Living and Dying,* poems from Rabindranath Tagore and Rainer Maria Rilke, and passages from the philosopher Paul Brunton. After telling a few stories about Vic, we fall into silence.

"The cremation is finished, Mrs. Mansfield," the mortician whispers two and a half hours after it began. My mind is quiet. Just as it was when Vic lay dying. Just as it was in Sankara's presence in India.

∽ ∾

When we return home, David, Anthony, and I are restless and edgy. I want to go upstairs and cry, but they decide to do what Vic and I taught them to do when times are hard. They plan a project. So instead of complaining or falling apart, the three of us plant tomatoes, peppers, and green beans, sweating in the heat of a long June evening.

"You're planting too much food for one woman to eat," I tell them.

"We'll be around a lot, and you can give food away to your friends," they insist, plugging another tomato plant in the ground and smacking in the stake.

"You're right," I agree. "Since your dad doesn't need me anymore, it will be a good summer to share food with friends."

That night I sleep deeply for the first time in many weeks. When I wake up at five, birds are singing morning serenades. *Where are you, Vic? Where did you go?*

Four days later, we sweat in tropical heat at Vic's memorial service. I suggest everyone wear casual summer clothes, just what Vic would have wanted to wear. My community of Wisdom's Goldenrod friends organizes the service, prepares a vegetarian feast, and decorates the meditation center library with the flower arrangements that continue to appear at my door. Vic's cousins arrive from Connecticut. There is a contingent from Colgate University where Vic taught.

The Venerable Tenzin Gephel from the Buddhist Namgyal Monastery in Ithaca leads us in prayers. I am not Buddhist in a formal sense and neither was Vic; but he was devoted to the Dalai Lama, taught a class on Tibet for twenty years at Colgate, wrote about Buddhism and physics, and often taught at Namgyal.

"Don't let people make me sound like a saint," Vic said a few months ago. This was his only request for his memorial service. As I listen to people read sacred poems and give moving tributes to Vic and his virtues, he sounds suspiciously angelic.

Our friend and doctor Michael Eisman stands up with a folded piece of plaid Indian cloth in his hand. His eyes are sad, but he has an impish smile. Michael pushes his thick dark hair away from his damp forehead and begins.

"Vic, Elaine, my wife Harriet, and I traveled to Kanchipuram, India, in March of 1990 to spend two weeks in the presence of Sankaracharya," Michael tells everyone. "Soon after we arrived, Vic and I received a surprise invitation to the monthly meeting of the Kanchipuram Rotary Club. This sounded too interesting to miss, but our luggage was lost between London and Madras, it was 90 degrees, and we had nothing to wear. So, we went shopping."

"'Bigger shirts,' we insisted as a circle of fine-boned Indian clerks gathered around us at the clothing store."

"'Final size, final size,' the clerks yelled, until we got it that there were no bigger shirts and no pants that would fit us either. Compared to South Indians, we were big guys." While he tells the tale, Michael wraps the brown checked cloth around his hips, spinning and grinning, tucking in the hanging edges of the cloth. "So, we went to the meeting in precariously wrapped Indian *dhotis* or skirts and cotton shirts so tight that the buttons popped open."

"The Indian businessmen wore impeccably tailored three-piece suits, crisply ironed white shirts, silk ties, and wing-tipped leather shoes. Along with our *dhotis* and bursting shirts, I wore my beat-up Nikes and Vic wore a pair of petite Indian sandals that kept falling off his feet. The businessmen did not mention our clothing, but politely asked us about our impressions of India."

Part of me watches Michael from a distance, wondering if comedy is acceptable on a day like this. I remember how Vic loved this story about India and how he called Michael "Swami Nike." It's a relief to laugh.

At the end of the service, after more serious readings and celestial music, my sons David and Anthony and a few of their friends go outside for a "chain saw salute," their woodsman's version of a twenty-one-gun salute with four chain saws roaring and belching smoke. Vic tended our forest and cut our firewood. From the time they were toddlers, David and Anthony loved being in the woods with their dad. When the chain saws roar, I imagine Vic roaring with them.

When the service is over, Anthony leaves to catch a flight to his home in California and David begins his long drive to North Carolina.

"It's OK if you leave," I assured them when we discussed our plans for this week. "I have to get used to living alone. No use delaying the inevitable." They need to return to their own worlds, talk to friends outside the pressure cooker of the family cancer crisis, and get a little distance from each other and me. I need to breathe in solitude and silence and drop down into my exploding heart.

I leave Wisdom's Goldenrod, the center where Vic and I meditated and took philosophy classes for over thirty-five years, and drive south on the two-lane highway overlooking Seneca Lake's vineyards. The largest of the Finger Lakes, Seneca is only two miles across but runs north and south in a forty-mile ribbon nestled between the hills. The shimmering sacred water calls me, but my dog has been alone most of the day, so I head uphill away from shore toward home.

"It's you and me, Daisy girl. Just you and me," I croon to my yellow Lab. Daisy wags her tail and looks up with unsure but hopeful eyes. She has smelled Vic's illness for a long time and must sense his death. Her brown eyes ask, *Now what?*

We do what we always do on hot summer evenings: I put on my wide-brimmed hat and hiking boots, put a handful of dog cookies in my pocket, and take Daisy for a walk. We move slowly through fields of lupines, thousands of deep purple spikes, self-seeded and spreading from wildflower beds Vic and I planted in recent years. In the forest, I admire delicate pink gaywings and wash my hot face and hands in the cool stream before we climb uphill to the red oak knoll where Vic and

I always found solace. I sit in green shade, lean into the largest red oak, listen to the forest birds sing what sounds to me like hopeful songs of love, and cry.

Daisy stays close, not letting me out of her sight. We hike to the highest point of the land for sunset and then return home to sit on the deck and watch the technicolor sky as the evening cools.

I'm glad to be without human company on the land Vic and I bought in 1972—alone with my dog, the bluebirds flying in and out of their nesting box, and my promising vegetable garden. Here, I can dive down into a slower place of sorrow that is new and numbing. *How am I supposed to withstand this pain and longing?* I ask the spirits that inhabit this land.

After dark, I climb the stairs to my bedroom. It's all as it was—the soft yellow walls, my maternal grandparents' bedroom set with my paternal grandmother's crocheted mandalas hanging behind it, my desk and computer and piles of books. I remove the candles, photos, statues, dried flowers, and white cloth from the altar on top of my dresser, sit on the bed, and look over the empty space.

Tibetan Buddhists believe that the after-death experience lasts forty-nine days, ending in a new incarnation. They perform special prayers and meditations for the one who has left and is moving toward a new life, but I don't care whether the seven-week time period is objectively related to what happens after death. I don't care whether Vic will be reincarnated at all. All I care about is focusing my love and grief for a limited amount of time and then finding a way to move on. No matter what happens to Vic, I need to release myself.

Following the advice of *The Tibetan Book of Living and Dying*, I dedicate a new altar to Vic. I lay a clean white cotton cloth over the dresser top, add a photo of Vic, and surround him with images of his teachers Anthony Damiani, the Dalai Lama, Paul Brunton, and Sankaracharya. I light a candle, wrap myself in my Indian silk, and sit before this altar for the first of many times, anchoring myself in my breath. I hear the last lines of the Buddhist Heart Sutra repeat persistently in my head: *"Gone. Gone. Gone beyond. Gone totally beyond. Oh, what an awakening!"*

Then I remember a conversation Vic and I had with Anthony Damiani soon after we met him in 1967.

"I'm terrified of death," Vic had confided.

"Widen your view," Anthony told him tenderly. "Mortality is universal. Human incarnation is a precious gift. Make the most of the time you have."

BEFORE

2

Organic vegetables and tofu.
Cancer anyway.

Vic comes down with a harsh lingering flu in January of 2006. He's an unusually vital sixty-five-year-old who lifts weights, exercises aerobically, and eats a nearly vegan whole foods diet. His dark circles and unending fatigue scare me. He's never been sick for this long. By late spring, he's a little stronger, although he's tired and his ankles are swollen.

"You should see Michael," I plead.

"Don't worry, E. I'm better. I'll have my usual physical in August."

I look at the dark circles and call Dr. Michael Eisman's office. When I tell Vic I made an appointment for him, he doesn't protest, so I know he's worried, too.

Michael calls Vic a few days after their appointment. Vic tells me Michael doesn't sound alarmed, but blood work shows an elevation in one type of white blood cell—possibly allergy, but possibly something worse. Michael suggests a follow-up, so Vic sets up an appointment in a few weeks when his teaching is over for the semester. I want this to move a little faster, but no one else seems in a hurry.

A week later, our close friend Fred is in town for a visit. I worked in Fred Weiner's office as a nutritionist for seventeen years, and he was our trusted family chiropractor before he moved to Arizona. Fred offers to give Vic a treatment. Probing and poking the way chiropractors do, Fred discovers enlarged lymph glands in Vic's groin. He calls Michael who immediately schedules a sonogram. After looking over the sonogram results, Michael calls an oncologist.

An oncologist? My throat tightens and my heart races when Vic says the word. How did we get from allergy to oncology? I pray there is some mistake.

"But he's always been the healthiest one of all of us," Michael's wife Harriet protests when she hears what's happening.

Rattled and confused, I buy a new spiral notebook and record every detail about Vic's illness, his diet, and what the doctors say. I also write down my feelings. I've practiced Jungian Active Imagination for many years and know it helps to express my fears in writing.

"I wish I could talk to Anthony," Vic says.

Our teacher Anthony Damiani died of cancer more than twenty years earlier, but I want to talk to him, too. When we were young and felt stuck in a hard situation, we counted on his wise advice.

We met Anthony Damiani in 1967 in the American Brahman Bookstore in Ithaca, New York. When we walked into the new store on State Street, a thick haze of cigarette smoke obscured a man standing at the back of the room. As we long-haired lovers walked toward him, his piercing black eyes sized us up like a coach looking for recruits for the soccer team. He was in his forties with bushy eyebrows and a full head of black hair slicked back with Brylcreem. He introduced us to Jungian psychology, meditation, and the philosopher Paul Brunton. Later he guided us in the study of Greek philosophy, Hinduism, Buddhism, and many western philosophers. We became vegetarians soon after meeting Anthony and helped build a meditation center that he named Wisdom's Goldenrod. He named it after a type of goldenrod flower, but it sounded more like a rod and gun club to me.

"He's gruff," a friend observed. "He smokes and plays loud opera, the same aria over and over again."

I understood her objections, but Eros had hit his mark. I wanted to learn everything Anthony had to teach me.

"Did you get that point?" Anthony asked after reading a passage from Plotinus about sculpting and perfecting the soul.

I got the point. My chattering mind grew still when I meditated in his presence and he opened my mind with new ideas about the spiritual life. My heart soared when he played Wagnerian arias or Barber's *Adagio for Strings*. I wanted to polish and refine my soul.

∽ ∾

"It's likely some type of lymphoma," a local oncologist tells us. "Most lymphomas are treatable. We'll do a bone marrow biopsy to see what you have."

I cling to the word treatable like a life preserver. After weekend talks with Fred and Michael, I'm getting used to the word cancer. *Please. Please let it be treatable.*

"Let's not tell anyone until we get a diagnosis," Vic suggests as we drive out of the medical building parking lot. I know he wants to protect everyone, but my parents kept my dad's kidney disease a secret when I was a kid. It was the way they handled illness in the 1950s, plus privacy around difficult issues was my mother's style. As a child, I felt distanced and confused by their secrecy.

"I need to tell David and Anthony and our friends," I tell Vic. "I don't want to do this on my own like my mother did. I need support. I think you do, too."

"You're right," Vic agrees. "I keep hoping this mess will disappear, but that doesn't look likely."

On the way home, we stop at GreenStar Natural Foods Market in Ithaca, see two close friends in the parking lot, and tell them about our visit to the oncologist. When they give us teary hugs, I know we've made the right choice.

"What do you need?" friends from the women's mythology class ask me when we meet one Sunday afternoon. We're taking a break from class this summer after studying mythology together for twenty years. At one time, there were more than a dozen in the class—teachers, psychologists, a psychiatrist, massage therapists, a librarian, and other women affiliated with Wisdom's Goldenrod—but a few women have moved and others could not continue.

"I need to feel close to all of you and work on a myth," I tell them.

In the past, our class studied Eros and Psyche, the Greek goddesses, Dionysius, Eastern European and Asian fairytales and myths, and most recently Inanna's descent to the underworld to receive initiation into the mysteries of Death. While we're searching for a new story, a class member living in Cambridge sees *Sonnets to Orpheus* by Rainer Maria Rilke in the window of the Harvard Book Store. She suggests we study Orpheus and Eurydice.

Orpheus was a musician, poet, and prophet in ancient Greek mythology whose music soothed and elevated all who listened. After his wife Eurydice died, he traveled to the underworld to play his lyre, sing his lament, and convince the gods to release Eurydice from death. His wish was granted but he was told not to look back at Eurydice until they were in the Light. Fearing that she wasn't behind him, Orpheus looked back and lost his love to Death.

We soon realize that we love the poetry as much as the myth, so Rilke's sonnets become our text. I fall in love with the mystical poetry. One of my favorite collections is *In Praise of Mortality* as translated by Anita Barrows and Joanna Macy. The class meets every other Sunday for three hours so we have time to check in with each other, explore the wisdom of the myth, read a sonnet, and paint images from the sonnets that move us—a willow tree, a peach, a sky of constellations, or a sarcophagus.

As Vic and I visit doctors and wait for a diagnosis, I absorb Rilke's message that each moment contains birth and death, beginnings and endings. Rilke praises the impermanence and the beauty of the natural world and teaches that we humans are part of the natural cycle. I know these truths from philosophy, but Rilke's poetic images give me an experience of the heart and a heightened appreciation of the preciousness of each moment. Vic and I are living; both of us are dying.

> Ah, the knowledge of impermanence
> That haunts our days
> Is their very fragrance.[2]

∽ ∾

A few days later, I drive Vic to the hospital for the biopsy.

"You can wait in the waiting room," a nurse tells me.

"I'm coming with him," I tell her. She places a chair next to the table where I watch my stoic husband writhe through the procedure. As he struggles to hold still, I cry silent tears and say my mantra inwardly as I always do in tough situations. *Om Mani Padme Hum. Om Mani Padme Hum.*

"I'll let you know the results in a few days," the oncologist says after the biopsy. "Sorry it hurt so much. I guess I didn't use enough lidocaine."

We wait, two days, three days, through the weekend. We are tender with each other, tiptoeing through a minefield of helpless fear. We take long walks in the woods, our pace slowed by the sense that nothing matters except this terrible threat. We remind each other to breathe.

On Monday, Vic calls the oncologist again, but the doctor doesn't call back. He doesn't return Vic's calls on Tuesday and Wednesday. I am furious and frightened by Vic's escalating symptoms. His nose runs, his eyes itch, and he wheezes. His skin is red and puffy. The nodes in his neck stand out like a map of the lymph system.

On Friday, I drive Vic to see Michael who calls the oncologist while we're there. That evening, the oncologist calls Vic at home. We've decided that I should record every detail, so I get on the other line.

"I sent the tissue sample to five labs and no one can identify it," the oncologist says.

"Why didn't you tell me?" Vic asks, trying not to sound as hostile as he feels. "You're leaving me out here on a spit."

"I thought you were feeling OK, but I guess you've gotten worse since I saw you. I wanted to call after I had a diagnosis."

We no longer trust this oncologist, so I call my brother Jim, who is dean of academic affairs at Harvard School of Public Health. He asks a colleague about the best lymphoma doctors in the northeast and follows up by email even though it's Labor Day weekend. His friend suggests the head of Oncology at Strong Hospital in Rochester and offers to get Vic an appointment. Even with all this help, we have to wait ten days.

While we wait and worry, I focus on the healing power of food. As I'm a nutritionist, this is a natural place to begin. Vic has a severe dairy allergy, so maybe, just maybe, cross my fingers, he's reacting to soy or wheat or peanuts. By now, this phantom has been lurking in his body for six months, slamming him with mysterious symptoms, then going underground before showing up again. I understand the desperation that drives sick people to small Caribbean islands where mysterious concoctions are pumped into their veins.

Not this. Please, not this. I beg and bargain as I create new dishes without wheat, soy, nuts, dairy, or tomatoes. Another part of me, wiser and closer to the heart, prays to endure whatever comes.

"Please, just tell me if you know what disease I have," Vic interrupts before the polite introductions are finished. We're sitting in a small windowless exam room at Strong Hospital with Dr. Richard Fisher and his teaching fellow Dr. Jeanna Walsh. We've already glimpsed our future in the crowded waiting room full of bald skinny people, some in wheelchairs, some working on a jigsaw puzzle laid out on a central table, most waiting their turn with closed, resigned faces.

"Yes, our pathologist identified the cancer from the bone marrow tissue. I'm sorry but it's a difficult one," Dr. Fisher says, his steady voice experienced in delivering bad news.

We're so relieved to hear that Dr. Fisher has a diagnosis that we ignore the difficult part. Vic's illness has a name: AITL (Angio-Immunoblastic T-cell Lymphoma), a rare cancer usually seen as a secondary cancer after radiation therapy. Other than radiation therapy, there are no known causes and Dr. Fisher has never seen it in someone who seems so healthy. AITL is incurable—a heart-stabbing word—but Dr. Fisher says they'll try a chemotherapy plan used for other types of lymphoma and hope for the best. I write furiously in my notebook, taking down every detail.

"Tuesday is the day we give chemotherapy to lymphoma patients," Dr. Walsh tells us as she fills out a treatment schedule for the coming months.

"Oh, God," Vic groans. "I have to wait another week?"

"We thought you might feel that way," she says reassuringly, "so we scheduled your first treatment in three days. The next treatment will be two and a half weeks later on a Tuesday and then every three weeks after that."

I watch Vic's face, wondering what he'll do.

"I'm sorry, but I can't have chemotherapy on that Tuesday," he says without hesitating.

"Really? You're kidding me," the nurse says.

"No, I'm serious. That day doesn't work."

"Just a minute," the nurse says, shaking her head in disbelief. "I'll get the doctor."

"Will it matter if I wait an extra week for the second chemotherapy?" Vic asks Dr. Fisher.

"I don't know. Probably not. What's happening?"

"Our community is seeing the Dalai Lama in Buffalo," Vic explains with tears in his voice. "It's my chance to give him a draft of the book I've just finished. He's writing an introduction. I need to go."

"It's important to do what you feel you have to do, so we'll delay the second chemo a week," Dr. Fisher decides, patting Vic's shoulder awkwardly.

My heart sinks as I hear what sounds like advice to a dying man.

We've been connected to the Dalai Lama since he made his first visit to the United States in October of 1979. Sidney Piburn, one of Anthony Damiani's students, had traveled to Dharamsala, India, to visit the Tibetan community-in-exile in the late 1970s. During one of his visits, Sidney had an audience with the Dalai Lama and invited His Holiness to visit our meditation and philosophy center.

Anthony hesitated when Sidney first proposed this visit. Anthony was wary of formal religion. He felt that taking any particular religious vow would tie him to the limitations of that religion rather than allowing him to explore the universal truths found in all traditions. For his own mysterious reasons, Anthony decided to welcome the Dalai Lama.

As we waited at the Ithaca airport for the arrival of the private plane carrying the Dalai Lama, Anthony's tailored off-white suit and tan overcoat startled me. I usually saw Anthony's tall broad-shouldered body in baggy khakis or a toll-taker's uniform since he worked nights on the New York State Thruway to support his family. He said there wasn't much traffic in the middle of the night and he liked the time for study.

Vic, our two young sons, and I stood outside with around fifty of Anthony's students behind a tall mesh fence that bordered the runway. Through large windows behind us, I watched Anthony inside the small private hangar. He was tight-jawed and serious, standing with his wife Ella May, Sidney, and one relaxed sheriff. Anthony, an avid coffee drinker, was preparing to offer the Dalai Lama welcoming tea, Tibetan style.

There was an expectant hush when the cabin door of the plane opened and dropped to the ground to create a stairway. A slender bald Asian man in his forties descended the stairs, tugging his maroon cloak over his left bare shoulder to protect against the October chill. He smiled and waved at us, but turned away and walked under the wing of the plane. Tipping his neck back, he looked up at the wing flaps and jiggled them vigorously with both hands, watching the motion with a studied look of curiosity. Then he turned toward us, his dark eyes sparkling, face open with wonder, he laughed with childlike delight. I laughed, too. Everyone laughed. We couldn't help it.

Two of Anthony's students who lived near Wisdom's Goldenrod vacated their home for the Dalai Lama and a few attendants. The rest of the Tibetans stayed in the main buildings at the meditation center. The security detail was miniscule—one county sheriff, one tall bodyguard wearing sunglasses and a trench coat, and a huge gentle man called "Tiny" who had met the Dalai Lama the week before in New York City and designated himself a bodyguard.

Besides local events at the center and in Ithaca, the Dalai Lama's visit included a lecture at Syracuse University and a trip to the Onondaga Indian reservation to visit tribal leaders. Anthony's students were in charge of transporting the Dalai Lama to each event. The men in the group jostled for months, hoping to drive or sit in the passenger seat. There would be no women drivers or passengers—perhaps because we were dealing with celibate monks, but also because there was a male hierarchy around Anthony. I wanted Vic to put his name in the hat. Vic was one of Anthony's closest students, and if he had prestige in this community, then so did I; but Vic quietly refused to join the competition and did not ask to be a driver.

On the last day of his four-day visit, the Dalai Lama met with a group of about twenty children and their parents in our newly built library that he had dedicated a few days before. He beamed as the unusually attentive and well-behaved little ones sang an old Irish song to bless him:

> May the long time sun shine on you,
> all love surround you,
> and the clear light within you
> guide your way home.

The Dalai Lama chanted Tibetan prayers and sat in silence for a few minutes. The children each chose one flower from a basket of white and yellow blossoms and presented it to His Holiness. He inspected each flower and handed it to an attendant, bowed to each child with his hands palm to palm, sometimes reaching out to pat a chubby hand or chuck a chin, smiling and laughing, looking deeply into each child's eyes. The children bowed back, subdued by the solemnity of the simple ritual.

On that day, I fell in love with the Dalai Lama. His Holiness was more interested in learning about what Anthony and his students were studying than in converting anyone to Buddhism, so my teacher seemed to fall for him, too.

In the fall of 1984, although Anthony was wasting from cancer, he endured a trip to Middlebury, Vermont, where he had a private meeting with the Dalai Lama. After their talk, the two teachers entered the room where a few hundred of Anthony's students waited. My heart filled with despair as Anthony, gray-skinned, thin, and weak, leaned heavily on the supportive arm of the robust Dalai Lama. After the meeting, I walked Anthony to his car with a few other students. He was too ill to talk.

"Thank you," I was able to say as I smiled into his sad eyes.

That day, Anthony asked the Dalai Lama to become the spiritual head of Wisdom's Goldenrod after his death. The Dalai Lama accepted. None of us knew just what that meant, but it was a comfort when Anthony died two days later.

"Chant *Om Mani Padme Hum* before you meditate together," the Dalai Lama advised us in the message he sent after learning of Anthony's death. Feeling like a lost sheep without my teacher of seventeen years, I felt grateful for his advice.

Three days after Vic's first appointment at Strong, we sit in a room of twenty tan vinyl recliners filled with patients hooked up to IV drips. There are old emaciated patients and young ones with stocking caps. Patients read, knit, watch TV, and huddle under warmed blankets. Vic's gray-flecked black hair looks out of place, but I know he won't have his curls for long. I don't care about his hair. I just want him to get better, but the patients in this room don't reassure me. Some people are alone, and some surrounded by family. A few look relatively healthy, but most are obviously and alarmingly ill. Looking around the room at the sick people and the nurses covered in protective clothing, I feel a rush of fear; but I pull my chair close to Vic, slide my hand into his, and take a deep breath.

Vic cries when the first drops of pastel fluid enter his vein.

"Don't be afraid," the nurse tells him, tenderly stroking his arm. "It will be OK. You'll get used to it."

"I know it sounds nuts, but I'm happy," he says. He opens his wet eyes and smiles up at her. "I'm crying because I'm finally getting help."

I do my best to visualize the Kool-Aid colored fluids passing into Vic's body as healing elixirs. I can't imagine ever getting used to this.

When we arrive home that afternoon, Barbara sits in her car in the driveway. Barbara is tall and blonde with blue eyes, ruddy cheeks, and Scandinavian robustness. We are both Anthony's students and members of the mythology class. She pulls a wicker basket out of the back seat of her car and hands it to me. The basket is neatly packed with covered bowls—green salad with dressing, a brown rice dish, stir-fried vegetables, and apple cake. Barbara smiles reassuringly, looks deeply into my eyes, and promises to call tomorrow to see if we need anything. Then she drives away.

That evening, Vic and I stroll along the paths in our fields, letting the familiar peace and beauty of our land soothe us. Late afternoon sunlight bounces off the wings of two white hawks who dance in the sky. Good omen, we hope.

Next morning, I wake up at dawn and snuggle next to Vic, silently inspecting his face and neck in the dim light. The swollen lymph glands look smaller, but I keep quiet, not wanting to give false hope or imagine improvements that aren't there.

"Do you think the lumps are smaller?" Vic asks after inspecting himself in the bathroom mirror. "They look smaller to me."

"Yes, I think so." We hug each other and let hope in.

In two days, just like magic, Vic's lumps disappear along with his allergy symptoms. I know it's naive to think this way, but maybe he'll be the first person to survive this disease.

During the five days of steroids that follow the chemotherapy infusion, I watch Vic's jaw clench and his eyes twitch. We were warned that prednisone causes agitation, sleeplessness, and emotional outbursts, but instead of raging, Vic pulls everything off the bookshelves in his office and sorts and boxes books for the annual Friends of the Tompkins County Public Library book sale. Then he empties his desk drawers, goes through the file cabinets, and throws out piles of accumulated papers. I cook his favorite soups and make appointments for him to see a chiropractor and a naturopath. I continue teaching a few clients how to exercise and eat for bone health, but my private practice is small, so I take time for long walks with Vic in the woods and appreciate the autumn colors. Nothing is more important than helping him survive.

Occasionally, I snarl at Vic's frantic energy or he growls because he can't sleep, but this seems like a good sign. A week ago, we were too scared to react to the small stuff.

"I can battle this monster because you're here with me," he tells me.

"I'm not going anywhere," I assure him with a hug.

A week after Vic's first chemotherapy, Lauren brings Geshe Kunkhen to our place for a walk and dinner. The Geshe is a chant master and visiting monk at Namgyal Monastery. Namgyal is the North American seat of His Holiness the 14th Dalai Lama, so many Tibetan monks and teachers come to Ithaca for extended stays. He has a shaved head and wears long maroon robes like most Tibetan monks. Vic became friends with Geshe Kunkhen when he and the Geshe taught together at a Buddhism and science conference at Cornell last winter. The Geshe knows about Vic's diagnosis and wants to help.

Lauren laughs and hoots when she sees us before wrapping her long arms around Vic and then me. We last saw each other a few days before chemotherapy started. She is a jeweler and wears a bright beaded necklace and earrings. I'm wearing silver earrings she made.

We walk south on a wide trail that leads from our house to the woods, Vic and I on either side of the Geshe. A warm wind caresses our faces and ripples through the Geshe's robes. The fields are the colors of Tibetan monks' robes, wind-blown goldenrod flowers swaying over an undercover of maroon dogwood leaves.

"This color every year?" the Geshe asks in halting English, his eyes gleam with delight.

"Every year," I tell him.

We walk down a moss-covered path under mature oaks, heading for what we call the red oak knoll, a small hill topped with one of the most magnificent oaks in our forest. This is the spot where Vic and I come to pray and find solace and where we imagine our ashes will be scattered. Knowing nothing about our unique relationship to this wooded hill, the Geshe abruptly drops to the earth and sits in meditation posture facing west. The late afternoon sun dapples his body and the earth under him with leaf-filtered light. He begins chanting. *Aummmmmm.* Long impossibly deep base notes seem to emanate from the earth, harmonized by middle tones and high keening overtones echoing off the treetops, all three sounds coming from one Tibetan throat. Lauren, Vic, and I drop to the forest floor around him, stunned and silenced. The chanting continues for half an hour, until the Geshe's voice drops off into a falling sound that goes deep and deeper into the bones. Then he rises as suddenly as he sat and walks down the trail as though nothing unusual has happened.

"What were you chanting?" Vic asks when we are back in the field.

"Chanting for Dakinis. Earth suffer. Dakinis suffer. Chant help forest

Dakinis be strong. We help them. They help you." Geshe was chanting to the local healing powers of this forest that Vic has tended for thirty-five years—the Dakinis, goddesses, tree spirits, angels, or whatever names we humans give this ineffable feminine life-force.

We walk back to the house, listening to crows, sacred birds of Tibet, call back and forth from the hedgerows. Inside after sunset, Geshe shows little interest in dinner. He wants to teach us a Tibetan Medicine Buddha healing practice.

I draw back, unsure about this. Tibetan Medicine Buddha? Is he going to ask me to chant Tibetan words or take part in religious rituals I don't understand? Our teacher Anthony taught that it was a mistake to limit ourselves to any one religion, but I keep quiet. Vic's diagnosis is dire. He needs something to hold, something to believe in. We both need to be receptive to whatever healing forces come to us. Geshe has no doubt. Maybe I can catch a ride on his faith.

"First see Medicine Buddha in mind," he instructs.

"I don't know what the Medicine Buddha looks like," Vic apologizes. Geshe glances at me with questioning eyes. I shake my head no. I don't know what the Medicine Buddha looks like either.

He pauses, thinking. "OK. You see Dalai Lama inside?"

"Yes," we nod.

"Good." Geshe smiles. "He your Medicine Buddha."

I'm sold. Geshe's practice leans on the essence of the matter, not the religious details.

"OK? You see Dalai Lama Medicine Buddha?"

"Yes."

Drawing a circle in the air, Geshe asks, "Around you see four Dakinis?" We don't know what Dakinis look like either.

"Four directions?" Vic suggests.

"Female powers of the earth?" I try.

"Good." Geshe says. "See that. Important part now. Medicine Buddha has bowl, blue healing water." He raises his cupped hands over the crown of his head as though he is baptizing himself with water held in his palms. "Pour it on top. Goes inside and outside body to feet. Wash sickness into earth."

"The sickness goes into the earth?" I ask.

"No worry. It's OK. Bodhisattvas under earth make enlightenment from sickness. No worry about sickness in earth. Clear water comes up and fills Vic with health. Good?"

"Good."

"Enough. Do every day. Do many times for chemotherapy. It works."

We don't ask how it works or on what level. It doesn't matter. We are grateful to receive a healing practice from this learned Geshe of the sacred voice. We do the Medicine Buddha practice daily, and during chemotherapy treatments, I imagine the color of the healing liquid as pastel yellow and pink, the colors of the medicines that drip into Vic's veins. I touch Vic's body with my hands or feet as he reclines in his La-Z-Boy chair during chemo. Together, we focus on the clear clean water rising from the earth to fill Vic with health. We don't demand that the practice cure Vic's body. It helps us accept the chemotherapy toxins as healing elixirs, and that's enough.

During that chemotherapy autumn, I take lessons from Rilke and from the brave women with scarves askew, bony men with smooth skulls, and angry teenagers with oversized baseball caps pulled over their baldness. Everyone in the chemotherapy room tries to balance the inescapable darkness with small positive experiences—a call from a friend, an afternoon soap opera, or music on their iPod. The nurses deliver maroon bags of blood and pink anti-nausea pills with smiles and pats. While they protect their bodies behind double layers of latex, they wipe tears, bring heated blankets, and give hugs. Their kindness makes this almost bearable.

Rilke's poetry helps me find strength as toxins enter Vic's veins.

> Let this darkness be a bell tower
> and you the bell. As you ring,
> what batters you becomes your strength.[3]

Rilke reminds me that death is always present, even in life's pleasure.

> Full round apple, peach, pear, blackberry
> Each speaks life and death
> into the mouth.[4]

Searching for life and light within the darkness of Vic's illness has become my spiritual practice.

◦⑤ ⑥◦

In October, after Vic's second round of chemotherapy, I dream that I stand on the upstairs landing of our home, wearing my nightshirt. I descend the stairs slowly in the darkness of night, my bare feet feeling their way down the wooden steps. At the bottom of the stairs, I stand at the doorway of the room where Vic sleeps, listening for the sound of his breathing. I hear his voice: "I don't want to die. I don't want to die."

Vic has been restless at night, so he sleeps downstairs. Even when he falls asleep next to me, he is gone by morning. When I wake up in the night, I sometimes walk downstairs, stand at the door of the room where he sleeps, and listen to him breathe. I need to make sure he is alive.

A few days after the dream, Vic and I attend a workshop with Robert Bosnak, a Jungian analyst and dream therapist who comes yearly to lead a weekend dream group in our area. In Bosnak's method, participants explore their dream images with the help of the group members' questions, creating an embodied waking experience of the dream events.

Imagining myself walking down the wooden stairs in total darkness, I experience solidity and safety in the soles of my bare feet. Hearing the resolute tone of Vic's dream voice fills me with courage to help him fight for life.

"I didn't know you were watching over me at night," Vic says after I share my dreamwork. "Thank you, E."

After the workshop, I add this dream image to my daily support. When I'm frightened or overwhelmed, I focus my energy in the soles of the feet and remember that something in me knows how to navigate this descent into darkness.

Vic manages eighteen weeks of treatment in a saintly frame of mind— grateful for help, resigned to the toxicity of chemotherapy and the agitation of prednisone, hopeful and steady. Now he wants to grow hair and run free. But during his first appointment in Rochester, he'd agreed to be part of a lymphoma study. After the last chemo, we learned Vic will be in the stem cell transplant group. The oncology nurses are elated. Vic is pissed off. He doesn't want more toxic medicine. I don't know what to think.

For ten days in December, Vic gives himself abdominal injections of Neulasta to entice his bone marrow to produce a glut of stem cells for harvesting. These stinging shots fuel his fury. He's also upset because he's submitted his book *Tibetan Buddhism and Modern Physics: Toward a Union of Love and Knowledge* to six publishers and received three rejections. The Office of the Dalai Lama in Dharamsala, India, had asked Vic to write a book on Buddhism and physics appropriate for Chinese-educated Tibetan students. Vic is not an initiated Buddhist, but he is a student of Tibetan Buddhism and, even though he's a physics professor, he teaches a class on Tibet.

I'm worn down by the clenched teeth and edgy nerves. I'm tired of circling my life around Vic's illness. Before he got sick, I was developing my exercise and nutrition consulting business, but that's on hold because I don't have energy for clients or classes when Vic needs so much attention. And now he will be in the hospital in Rochester for at least three weeks for the stem cell transplant. I want him to live. I want to do all

I can to support him. I also want my own life. It's a familiar conflict.

When I was twenty-one and fell in love with Vic, I walked away from graduate school without looking back. After David and Anthony grew up, I struggled to find my work in the world. In recent years, I found my niche, writing and teaching classes on bone health, but my work fades as Vic needs full-time support. I don't want to resent taking care of him, but resentment creeps in anyway, especially when he's irritable.

And the stem cell transplant protocol is irritating. More than regular chemotherapy treatments every three weeks, the transplant keeps life on hold. Admission to the transplant unit doesn't happen at a pre-scheduled date. Instead, patients wait in line for an opening. It reminds me of being pregnant and waiting for labor to begin. The packed suitcases sit by the front door.

"We'll have a bed for you tomorrow morning," a caller says on January 12. "Are you ready?"

No, I am not ready; not really. My list-making orderliness abandons me.

I can't do this. *You must do this.* I can't remember what I'm supposed to do. Relax. I don't want to do this today or ever. *You have no choice.*

I throw Vic's protein powder and supplements in a bag, fill the bird feeders, and water the houseplants. Vic gathers books, papers, and music. I want to cry, but there is no time for that, so instead I fuss about details that don't matter. By midnight, I'm ready.

At eight the next morning, a nurse from the transplant unit calls to tell us that the person who went home yesterday was readmitted in the night.

"Sorry. It was an emergency. We'll call on Monday with a new tentative date."

The weekend is outwardly quiet, but inwardly tense. We jump each time the phone rings, thinking that will be the call from Strong. Monday comes and goes. No phone call; no directions. We wait. Tuesday morning, ten o'clock, the phone rings.

"When are you arriving this morning?" the voice asks.

"Arriving? No one called us."

"Oh. Mary went on vacation this weekend. She must have forgotten to call you. When can you get here?"

"Can we come tomorrow?"

"We'll give the bed to someone else if you don't come today. When can you get here?"

"In four hours," I promise, two for last-minute preparations and two to drive.

I scamper through the house. *Where's that book I was reading last night? What did I do with my snow pants? Where are Vic's extra glasses?* Despite weeks of preparation, everything is misplaced and out of order.

"Stop!" Vic snarls. "It doesn't matter if we get there in four hours or five hours or tomorrow. It matters that we stay calm. You're driving me crazy. I'm driving you crazy. Calm down, E. We need to breathe."

We sit across from each other in the living room. When I remember to feel my feet planted on the floor and the Medicine Buddha in my heart, the tears I've held back for days break through the dam and soak my shirt. It would be easier to change my attitude and let go of my need to control the chaos, but I don't know how to do it. I only know how to be miserable and afraid. After my tears dry and Vic's agitation cools, we quietly finish packing.

On the way to Rochester, I sit in the passenger seat feeling small and ashamed. Vic drives below the speed limit to prove his point. When we arrive at the hospital, we stand in the parking garage and hold each other before going in. We forgive.

Eleven patient rooms surround the nurses' station at the stem cell transplant unit. The ward is a stainless steel, plastic, glass, and disposable paper isolation booth with a mind-deadening roar from air filtering fans. One hallway leads to the elevators and the outside world, an escape route for me, but off limits to Vic.

The high dose chemotherapy drip begins at ten p.m. Nurses advise Vic to drink water, eat lightly, and talk to the social worker or a nurse when he's upset. They also tell him to keep moving.

For the first few days, with his IV pole at his side, Vic walks on a treadmill that is tucked out of the way behind a refrigerator. I'm proud of how hard he tries to stay strong. He's a bald-headed hamster on an exercise wheel, but after he stumbles and falls, nurses put the treadmill off limits and he's reduced to slow walks circling the nurses' station. Sometimes I circle with him. The other ten rooms cloister eerily silent patients who rarely emerge into the circular hallway, but sometimes I meet the families in the kitchen area.

"I can't convince her to live, even for the sake of her baby," a haggard mom tells me, shaking her head with discouragement. Her twenty-five-year-old daughter is too depressed to move or eat.

A few rooms down, a year-old Mennonite baby is secluded with his family. I see the boy through open blinds of the door to the room. He clings to his mother's neck. Black clad Mennonite men and women come and go like shades, eyes averted.

"Will you put my casserole in the microwave?" the baby's black-capped grandmother asks me, holding out a glass pan. "I can't touch a microwave." I'm struck that a stem cell transplant is OK in her religion, but not a microwave and remember why I'm wary of religious rules.

Other than email, daily telephone calls with David and Anthony, and the rotating hospital staff, I am Vic's only human contact. I sleep at the American Cancer Society Hope Lodge, fifteen minutes away from the hospital. Hope Lodge, once a nunnery, has convent-style bedrooms and kitchen privileges for people who need housing while they or their family member undergo cancer therapy. The sunrise outside my bedroom window awakens me early so I have time to meditate. Late at night in the institutional kitchen, I cook bland vegetable soups for Vic and me to eat the next day. On the way to the hospital each morning, I stop at Wegmans to buy fresh whole grain bread for Vic and a blueberry muffin for me. I need comfort.

In the morning, Vic and I talk, read, and answer email from friends. After eating our soup, I pull on snow pants and hiking boots and spend an hour outside in the bitter January cold while Vic tries to sleep. I have discovered the Mount Hope Cemetery across the road from the hospital.

"Conveniently located," Vic quips.

Dedicated in 1838 as the first municipal non-religious cemetery in the United States, Mount Hope is full of majestic oaks and maples, spreading lilac bushes, and old evergreens. The narrow winding roads are plowed each day. Occasionally I see a Lycra-clad runner or someone tucked into a down parka walking a dog, but most days I walk alone beneath squawking flocks of crows and blue jays.

Each day, I venture a little deeper into the maze of winding roads, exploring nooks I haven't seen. I read the tombstones as I walk, moved by the children's graves. Gladys M. Perkins, March–July 1893. Earl F. Jones, 1899–1900. I rarely find anyone who lived as long as Vic's sixty-five years. Alfred Hall, 1863 to 1912. Forty-nine years old; an old man in 1912. Early in Vic's hospital stay, I leave an acorn at the gravestone of Frederick Douglas (1818–1895). A month into my explorations, tucked far from the hospital, I find the grave of Susan B. Anthony (1820–1906). She showed up, did her noble work, and then she died. That's the best any of us can hope for.

The stone monuments dusted with fresh lake-effect snow bring life to this place of death. As I walk through the cemetery, I remember Anthony Damiani's advice when facing the fear of death. Widen the view.

⤸ ⤷

Vic manages the first week with extreme fatigue, but none of the alarming side effects we were warned about. He's still eating a little, drinking a lot, and getting out of bed each day.

"You are the calmest spouse I've seen around here," the social worker who takes care of transplant patients and their families tells me. "It's terrific that you're managing the pressure so well."

"You can't see the chaos inside," I tell him.

But he's partly right. Vic isn't bedridden or shuttled to the emergency room in the middle of the night like many of the patients here. He tells me when he's anxious and I tell him when I'm scared. We have a pact to be straight about our feelings, a remnant of our 1960s encounter-group days when we learned to be honest with each other. Despite how lousy he feels, he still pats my bottom and caresses my hand.

At night, I leave Vic in the hospital and return to Hope Lodge where I first make soup and then call people I love. I phone David and Anthony and at least one of my close women friends every day. We often read Rilke lines to each other. In one late-night conversation, Barbara reads me the final three lines of the last poem in *Sonnets to Orpheus*. I write the mystical stanza with white chalk on black paper and post it on the door to my room.

> And if the world has ceased to hear you,
> Say to the silent earth: I flow.
> To the rushing water, speak: I am.[5]

I don't know exactly what the words mean, but they comfort me as I move in and out of my nun's cell. In this transplant world, it's easy to feel forgotten by the world. All I can do is flow and know that I am.

⤎ ⤏

We wait for Vic's white blood cell count to drop. In an autologous stem cell transplant, high dose chemotherapy kills all the white blood cells. When the white blood cell count is zero, the stem cells that were harvested and saved are infused into the patient. If all goes well, all cancerous lymphoma cells die and the body makes new healthy white blood cells.

They draw Vic's blood at 4:00 each morning, and by 8:00 nurses write the diving numbers on a chart on the wall. As the numbers drop, Vic frets.

"Without those frozen cells, I'm a dead duck. What if they misplace my stem cells? What if my body rejects them? What if they give me someone else's cells?"

"It'll be OK," I offer for the hundredth time. I'm worried, too, but not about losing Vic's stem cells. I'm worried about Vic losing his equilibrium.

"This could go wrong in a million ways. I'm a guinea pig and this may not work, but there is a chance," he reminds himself with a sigh. "I'm grateful for a chance."

"It's normal to be afraid," I assure him. My words don't help. Vic leans into me, just as the Mennonite baby clings to his mama, but when the aide takes his blood pressure, it's over the top.

"I can't control my thoughts," Vic moans. He doesn't have to tell me. He thinks he should be in control of his reactions because he's meditated for forty years, but I can read the panic in his face.

"Vic, please," I plead. "Your jaw is a rock and your blood pressure is soaring. Anyone would be frightened. The nurses have been trying to get you to take Ativan for days. Why not try it?"

"I don't want drugs for anxiety. I want to feel what I'm going through."

"Vic, your immune system is on its last legs. We know your stem cells will save you, but we can't convince your body of that. Your body thinks it's dying."

"You would be freaked, too!" he pops back with a defensive edge in his voice, and then his shoulders slump forward.

"E, the head nurse told me that every patient here is taking anti-anxiety drugs to deal with the panic reaction. She says I should accept any help I can get."

"So what's wrong with that, Vic? What could be wrong with accepting help?"

"I'm afraid of losing control of everything that's left. I might lose my mind."

"Hey, that's not a bad idea," I say with a grin. He doesn't smile. "Vic, I need you to do it for me. Forget your ideals and your aspirations.

Take the Ativan. It's exhausting to live on this ledge." Vic sighs, lies back on the bed, and closes his eyes. I sit at the table next to his bed and download email.

"I'll buzz the nurse," he says after a few minutes. "She'll be glad to hear from me."

A few hours later, the atmosphere in Vic's room takes on a soft glow. His blood pressure is lower and his jaw is loose. He listens to Verdi on his iPod and flirts with the idea of a nap. I work on my computer at the table next to his bed, writing to my women friends about his stubborn strength. When his hand reaches out to encircle my wrist, I move close to him and sit on the edge of the bed.

"I love you, Vic, but the heroic mode wears me out. Thanks for lowering your standards."

ം ഔ

Severely weakened, but still able to get out of bed, Vic slowly circum-ambulates the nurses' station day and night. He's not sleeping much, so he sometimes walks after midnight, sending healing prayers into the rooms of other transplant patients as he passes their closed doors. One night, he finds a woman in her thirties stitching a quilt under the harsh fluorescent light. In his usual style, he's curious about her situation and asks her what she's doing.

"It's a love quilt," she tells Vic. "A marriage quilt. I'm making it to renew my marriage, but my husband won't lie under it with me. We have one child with autism and our youngest son has lymphoma and is getting a stem cell transplant. He's sleeping now. I can't take the loneliness. My husband wants out."

Vic puts his hand on her hunched shoulder. She looks up in surprise and thanks him, blinking back tears. When he tells me the story the next morning, it's obvious that soothing this woman's suffering gave him a little distance on his own fear.

ം ഔ

Two weeks into Vic's hospitalization, friends drive to Rochester so we can have mythology class in the library at Hope Lodge. We read and discuss a Rilke sonnet and paint images from the poem. The sonnet gives me another lesson in mortality.

> . . . Orpheus, the conjuring one,
> Mixes death into all our seeing,
> Mixes it with everything.[6]

While we eat lunch, we talk about our lives, especially mine. When they leave for Ithaca in the afternoon, I drive to the hospital replenished.

Vic comes home seventeen days after his admission to the stem cell transplant unit, the fastest turnaround time the staff can remember. His white blood cell count soars after the stem cell infusion, and although he's anemic, he doesn't need the usual blood transfusions. We pile his computer, books, and clothes in the wheelchair and he pushes it to the car.

A few days later when I return home from grocery shopping, Vic waits by the front door, obviously upset and holding back tears.

"What's up?" I ask, afraid he has bad news about a blood test.

"Paul Cash phoned," Vic says in a quiet voice. Paul is Vic's agent and editor. "While I was getting the stem cell transplant, three more publishers turned down my book. They say they like it, but it's too difficult, or too personal, or too something. What's the point of this heroic struggle?" Vic shakes his head with sorrow. "I'm a dead man at a dead end."

∽ ∾

A week after Vic's release from the hospital, blood work confirms that Vic is doing remarkably well. As his body gets stronger, he dares to hope he will have time to see his book through to publication. Paul submits Vic's book to Templeton Press. Within days, the head editor calls to say it's perfect for Templeton. Vic and I cross our fingers.

In April 2007, three months after the stem cell transplant, Vic has eyelashes, wispy dark hair, and terrific energy. He's taking care of his body and meditating at least twice a day. I'm burned out and need a break from cancer and caregiving, so I sign up for a week-long Body/ Soul Rhythms workshop in Canada with Jungian analyst and author Marion Woodman. Marion has been my teacher for twenty years. She is in her late seventies and has been battered by ovarian cancer, but she still gives workshops with her assistants Mary Hamilton and Ann Skinner.

I love driving west on the New York State Thruway toward Rochester without Vic in the car. It feels even better when I drive past the exit to Strong Hospital and follow signs to the Niagara Falls bridge to Canada. I'm going somewhere, by myself, for myself. Vic doesn't need me.

The workshop is at Oakwood Resort on Lake Huron. The first afternoon, I settle into my private room, take a long walk on the sandy white beach along the lake, and have dinner with other women in the workshop. I know a few women from previous gatherings, but I'm more interested in having a retreat than in socializing. That night, I dream that a caged hummingbird is released into the wild.

The next morning, I get up early, meditate, and walk on the beach again. After the opening ritual, I find a chair in the semi-circle of forty women, open my notebook, and wait for the session to begin.

"Your husband is on the phone," a woman I've never met whispers in my ear. My heart thumps with fear as I follow her to the retreat office. Vic wouldn't disturb me during a retreat unless something terrible happened.

"I'm OK," Vic reassures me in a strong clear voice. "The nursing home just called to say that your mother stopped taking water and food. They think she's dying."

"Thank God it's my mom and not you," I tell him.

My ninety-one-year-old mother lives in a skilled nursing home ten miles from our home. She spent five years in an Alzheimer's home in Rochester before her elderly second husband asked me to take over her care six years ago. When she first lost her memory, she was fearful and clingy and I spent all the time I could with her, but now she is peaceful. She doesn't speak and hasn't known me or anyone for many years. She lies unresponsive in a fetal position with closed eyes. Once or twice a week, I feed her chocolate ice cream and spend an hour reading or singing to her or brushing her hair. Before Vic's illness, Mom was my main concern; but she's in a great place with kind caretakers, so now I see her often when Vic is doing well and spend less time with her when he isn't.

"Will you go to the nursing home to be with her, Vic?" I ask.

"I'm ready to go."

"In case she dies before I get there, take the white and blue blankets that I bought for her shroud."

I call the nursing home and talk to the head nurse.

"Your mom didn't eat yesterday and today she won't take fluids."

"Don't force her," I plead. "I'm in Canada, nine hours away. Should I start driving?"

"Wait until this afternoon," the nurse suggests. "If she dies quickly, you won't have time to get here, or she may linger for weeks. Call this afternoon. I'll know more."

During the morning workshop, I imagine my mother being released from her spent body, a tiny hummingbird released from its cage. When I return to my hotel room after the morning session, the phone message light is blinking.

"Your mom died this morning." Vic's voice on the machine is gentle and calm. "Call me when you can."

"Her breathing was so quiet it was hard to tell when life ended and death began," Vic assures me on the phone. "I held the crown of her head and enveloped her in love. Then, I sat next to her and meditated."

"Thank you, Vic," I whisper, weeping as much from relief as sorrow. Twelve years of Alzheimer's was an endurance test for everyone.

"I took photos so you could see how relaxed she was," Vic says. "There was no resistance."

❦   ❧

Marion doesn't join the evening session, but I tell the other women what happened.

"Are you leaving?" they ask.

"No, I'll stay. My mother is gone, and my husband is handling things."

"Are you OK? Do you need anything?"

"I need to be here with you and with Marion."

The leader of the evening session gathers the group into a circle and offers a prayer for the safe passage of my mother Iva May. We stand together holding hands. All eyes look expectantly at me, so I ask that each woman call her mother's name into the circle: "Iva May," I begin. Then I hear other women's voices calling out, "June, Carol, Betty Lynn, Jeanette . . ." Our mothers' names are prayers.

❦   ❧

"When is the funeral?" Marion asks the next morning.

Funeral? Wasn't last night enough? Mom doesn't have any living friends or relatives except my brother and me. Her husband died a few years ago.

"It's important to mark your mother's passing with a community ritual," Marion insists even though I haven't said a thing. "It's important to honor her, but it's essential for you."

During the remaining days of the workshop, I dance, paint, and write about the relief and sadness of my mother's death and the terror of Vic's illness. I feel closer to Marion than ever before, as though with the death of my biological mother, Marion has taken up the mantle of soul mother. She watches me closely.

"Are you OK?" she asks.

"My mom had Alzheimer's for many years," I remind her. "Losing her is simple compared to what is happening with Vic." Marion looks into my eyes, nods with understanding, and hugs me. Marion also has a long intimate marriage. She knows.

A month later, I invite a dozen women friends to join me on my mother's birthday. We sit on the deck at sunset, read poetry, watch hummingbirds sip sugar water at the feeder, and tell stories about our mothers. We end by speaking our mothers' names into the circle.

It's been nearly six months since Vic's stem cell transplant. It's been nine months since he was diagnosed with lymphoma. It's been more than a year since he felt lust.

We're seeing Dr. Fisher to get the results of the most recent PET-CT scan. Despite months of debilitating treatment, Vic has regained his vitality. He has a new crop of short dark curls on his head. He's once more the Vic who lifts weights, eats whole foods, and behaves like an Italian peasant. We're full of hope.

"There are some small active spots near your lungs on the scan," Dr. Fisher tells us in his grave doctor voice. We're sitting knee-to-knee in a small institutionally gray exam room at Strong Memorial Hospital. "We would rather they weren't there, but perhaps it's nothing. We'll have to wait and see."

Vic and I sit quietly, composing ourselves. We were praying for better news, praying to escape the jaws of death.

"I'm sorry, but I hope it's nothing. These things are hard to interpret," Dr. Fisher says, disappointment dripping from his words. "Do you have any questions?"

"Well . . ." Vic hesitates before plunging ahead. "I feel amazingly well, but I can't get an erection."

"Yes," Dr. Fisher smiles without any embarrassment. He's heard this one before. "This usually happens after stem cell transplant. The procedure does a job on the testosterone levels."

"I know, but is there anything to be done about it?" Vic asks. "I want to make love with my wife. I want to want to make love."

"Would you like to try Viagra?"

"Will it work?"

"It might. It's worth a try."

"Yes," Vic grins, glancing at me like a naughty teenager. "Let's try it. Why not?"

"Why not?" Dr. Fisher agrees.

Why not? My heart beats a little faster as Dr. Fisher pulls out his pad and writes a script for a large dose.

A few days later, Vic and I walk through our fields on a warm June evening, hold hands, admire the first bloom of lupines, and watch for hawks. Then we sit on the deck with glasses of Pinot Noir. Vic goes inside and returns, impishly laying one large four-sided sea-blue pill on the table between us. Aphrodite's color, I think. Vic swallows the pill with red wine. We joke that we are worshipping Priapas—the ancient Greek fertility god of fruit, vegetable crops, and male genitals who is depicted with an elephant-sized permanent erection. We laugh, but this is a sacrament. It's been a long, harsh famine.

We spend half an hour undressing and exploring each other's bodies, savoring each other's sweetness and inhaling each other's salty flavors. His warm soft lips kiss my face with the patience of a man who faces mortality. Our first kisses taste of tears and the knowledge that our time together is finite.

Vic's erection lasts and lasts. My unhurried body warms, grows moist and welcoming. Lying on our sides, he enters me from behind, his hands secure my hips and his belly presses into my buttocks. He holds a breast in each hand as he kisses the back of my neck. We move together with long slow thrusts, breathing in rhythm. He is my ideal lover—relaxed and patient.

We so want to please each other, and we do.

3

Monster snarls. The warrior battles on.

Vic spends the spring and summer of 2007 wrapping up final edits with Templeton Press and rebuilding his strength with exercise and healthy food. The release date for the book is March 2008, so he organizes a spring tour in the US, Canada, and Mexico. He also signs up to teach his course on Tibet at Colgate in the fall. With his cancer at bay, I return to giving private exercise and nutrition consultations and organize a series of women's health classes in Ithaca for fall.

We do not once hear doctors use the word "remission." I try not to dwell on cancer, but it seeps into every thought and plan. The word "incurable" hovers over our heads along with those spots on the scan. Everyone says Vic looks terrific, especially his doctors, and the blood work is good; but I'm unsettled by the grief and seriousness in Vic's eyes. My eyes mirror his feelings.

In September 2007, eight months after the stem cell transplant, Vic commutes to Colgate one day a week to teach the Tibet class. Driving home on a hot afternoon, he glances down at his bare thighs and sees an angry rash that wasn't there in the morning. He shows me the red splotches when he gets home.

Cancer! My gut knots with fear. Then my mind floods with reasons why it can't be. He's been well for six months. He has hair and is strong in weightlifting and aerobics. This blotchy rash looks nothing like the first cancer symptoms a year and a half ago.

Over the next few days, we are tender with each other as the rash worsens and a general swelling begins. On the fifth day, we see Dr. Jonathan Friedberg, a lymphoma specialist at Strong Hospital who was Vic's doctor during the stem cell transplant and will be his primary oncologist from now on. Vic looks like he's been dipped in boiling water. His hands are so swollen that he can't type on his computer keyboard and his feet don't fit in shoes.

"Poor thing," Dr. Friedberg mutters as he probes Vic's groin and underarms with his delicate long-fingered hands and runs his fingers gently over Vic's red thighs and back.

"Maybe it's a drug reaction," I propose, hoping for his agreement.

"Maybe," Dr. Friedberg says with a raised eyebrow, "but let's do a skin biopsy to make sure." His half smile is not reassuring.

My belly clenches with dread as we make our way to Dermatology.

"This is definitely a reaction to the Bactrim that you're taking," a bouncy dermatologist tells us. "I see it all the time with sulfa drugs. You don't need a biopsy." We grab hold of her story like a lifeboat, but just to make sure, I ask her to contact Dr. Friedberg to see if he agrees. She calls his cell phone number repeatedly, but he doesn't answer. Around six p.m., she sends us home with a huge jar of cortisone cream, a bucket of hope, and no biopsy.

The cortisone cream makes the rash disappear, but not the swelling. The next week, we visit Dr. Friedberg again. He is usually a mild-mannered fellow, but his face turns fury red when he hears that the dermatologist didn't do a biopsy.

"Find out what happened," he orders his nurse. "What number was she calling? I was available." He groans when he hears that the dermatologist called the wrong area code.

"Stop using the cortisone cream and the Bactrim for two weeks," he tells Vic, "and if the rash returns, we'll get a biopsy. If there is still no rash in two weeks, we'll biopsy a lymph gland. I can't treat you without a clear diagnosis. I'm afraid this is lymphoma, but so far I'm only guessing."

We wait on edge. It's been almost a month since the rash first appeared. Now Vic has a cough and a constantly running nose. He is weak and dizzy and his body continues to swell. Dr. Friedberg prescribes diuretics for symptom relief until the rash reappears.

"My heart feels funny," Vic complains in a weak voice on Sunday afternoon when I return home from mythology class. I check his pulse. His heart rate is fast and with long arrhythmic pauses. Alarmed, I call our close friend Gita Ramamurthy who is a psychiatrist and internist.

"He needs an EKG," Gita says, so I call Michael Eisman who advises me to take Vic to the Cayuga Medical Center emergency room. Michael says he'll call ahead to tell the hospital what is needed and will check in with Vic in the morning. I swallow my panic, toss Vic's toothbrush and a change of underwear in a bag, and drive him to the hospital.

Gita meets us in the ER, holds our hands, and waits with us while doctors decide what to do. The EKG is abnormal, and Vic is admitted. The next morning, a cardiologist suggests IV diuretics.

"I've reacted strangely since starting oral diuretics a few days ago," Vic tells him. As his primary physician, Michael Eisman tells the cardiologist the same thing and suggests finding a different option; but this new doctor is sure that the abnormality is caused by fluid around Vic's heart and that diuretics will solve the problem. The cardiologist calls Dr. Friedberg and gets an OK. Trapped without another choice, we fearfully agree. I hold Vic's hand as a nurse hooks up an IV and the diuretics begin to drip into his body. *Om Mani Padme Hum.*

᭰ ᭳

An hour after the infusion begins, Vic seems OK. So I drive into Ithaca to pick up his elderly mother Virginia so she can visit her son. When

Virginia and I enter the hospital room, Vic has a yellow-green pallor and is too sick to chat, so his frightened mother asks me to take her home.

"He's in good hands," I assure Virginia during the five-minute drive to her apartment, even though I don't believe it. I'm grateful that David and Anthony will arrive tomorrow. Vic and I bought tickets for the family to see the Dalai Lama who is visiting Ithaca this week, so they had already planned to come home.

I push through the inner glass doors of the hospital lobby around five p.m. and find my way down convoluted hallways to the intensive care unit. This is the only place they had a bed last night. There is a huge commotion in one of the rooms. People shout and run in and out. Buzzers shriek. *Some poor soul must be dying. Where is Vic's room?* There are at least ten people milling around in the hall and another ten rushing around inside one of the rooms.

"Is the man in this room your husband?" a woman I've never seen before asks quietly. She slides her arm firmly through mine and pulls me away from the door. I don't budge.

"What's happening?" I ask, shocked into the realization that Vic is the center of this commotion.

"Your husband is having problems. Come with me. You're not allowed in there."

"Is he alive?" I ask, edging through the crowd so I can look through the doorway.

"I don't know."

"I'm going in. I won't make a fuss."

She pulls my arm in protest, but I ignore her. Defeated, she follows me into the room. I stand against the wall, careful not to get in the way. Vic is an unconscious rag doll, legs askew, head limp, naked. I can't tell if he's breathing. Doctors and nurses shove needles into his arms and thighs and tubes in every orifice. In a flash, he's intubated and catheterized. I'm horrified by their roughness, but they're in a hurry. The heart monitor line is flat. A male nurse holds paddles over Vic's chest.

"Stand back!" he yells. He puts the paddles on Vic's chest and fires.

Vic's body convulses. I tremble. The monitor stays flat. The nurse shocks him again, and the line jumps to a wave.

"We have a heartbeat," someone yells.

Doctors and nurses glance at me with irritation. I ignore them and move to the foot of the bed, slipping my hands under Vic's bare feet, praying for surrender, praying for gentle passage, praying for I don't know what. *Thy Will Be Done. Maybe it's time for him to die. Maybe this is the path of least suffering.*

The heartbeat on the monitor stays steady, and the panic in the room subsides. Nurses clean Vic's incisions and remove spots of blood from his face and belly. Vic's body is here, but he is not.

"It's lucky he was already in the hospital," a flush-faced doctor tells me. "We had him intubated a few minutes after his heart stopped. There won't be any brain damage."

"What happened?" I ask in a steady voice that must be coming from someone else.

"His heart started fibrillating and then he went into cardiac arrest."

Nurses pick up the sheets from the floor and drape Vic's naked body with a hospital gown. I hold his feet, shocked into calm. The woman next to me asks if I need anything.

"I just want to stand here," I tell her. I have to touch Vic. I have to feel his warm skin. I have to watch the heart monitor.

Eventually, I move to the side of the bed and slip my left hand under Vic's limp right hand. With my right hand, I call David on my cell.

"I'll be in Ithaca in two hours," David says. "I'll come to the hospital."

I call Anthony who is catching a plane tomorrow morning. I call our friend Janet Wylde who has been giving Vic healing massage for years and ask her what energy points to hold for the heart.

"Steve and I will be there in ten minutes," Janet says. I met Steve Smolen when he was a student at Colgate in 1975. Thinking of him reminds me that Vic is supposed to take his Tibet students to see the Dalai Lama the day after tomorrow

Before I have time to catch my breath, Vic's heart goes berserk again.

I cringe as his body convulses under the paddles, but his heart resumes a normal rhythm.

"Why is this happening?" I ask the nurse. He shrugs his shoulders and shakes his head sadly, a man who has seen too much.

I hold Vic's right hand and begin beating a slow rhythm into his palm. Ba-boom, ba-boom, ba-boom. His heart has forgotten the tempo. Maybe I can help it remember. Ba-boom, ba-boom, ba-boom. It's hard to keep my eyes off the heart monitor.

When Janet arrives, she stands across the bed near Vic's left shoulder, tears rolling down her cheeks. She cradles the nape of his neck with her right hand, touching his chest with her left. Steve sits on the floor and quietly makes phone calls to our friends.

Buzzers blare. The nurse rushes in, a blur of blue scrubs.

"Stand back."

One shock. Flat line. Two shocks. A wave.

"Keep doing what you're doing," the nurse encourages. "It's good to touch him."

Janet steps back to Vic's side and I resume tapping. Ba-boom, ba-boom, ba-boom.

Lauren arrives. So do Michael and Harriet Eisman. David walks into the room and wraps me in his arms. In the next hour, a dozen or more people slip into the room like whispers and sit on the floor to meditate, surrounding Vic's bed with quiet. Over the next few hours, there are more cardiac arrests and many more shocks. I lose count.

"How long will they shock him?" I ask Michael.

"Until it doesn't work," he says, hugging me. Ba-boom, ba-boom, ba-boom.

Lauren moves close and takes over tapping Vic's hand. Janet doesn't move from Vic's side. Our friend Gail holds his feet. I step back from the bed and sit next to David, leaning into him. There are two circles of protection around my beloved, three women holding his body, and outside that, the meditators who create a sacred space in this metallic and plastic room. Waves of exhaustion pour over me. I close my eyes, pray, and wait. Ba-boom, ba-boom, ba-boom.

Before midnight, Vic's heart settles. We dare to hope he will not die, at least not tonight.

For a few hours, I sleep fitfully in a lounge chair pulled next to Vic's bed in the ICU. When I open my eyes to a pink dawn, Lauren is sitting beside me, meditating with open eyes focused on Vic. Other friends went home late and David fell asleep in his truck in the hospital parking lot.

"Go home and rest," I tell Lauren. "I'm OK." She's seeing the Dalai Lama today and tomorrow and is helping with the event. I give her our tickets for today's lecture and ask her to give them away.

Lauren and I cling to each other for a moment, and then she leaves, glancing apprehensively at Vic's unconscious body. Soon David shows up, groggy and somber. Steve drops by the hospital room on his way to see the Dalai Lama at Cornell University. Vic planned to take students from his Tibet class to see the Dalai Lama tomorrow at Ithaca College. Steve offers to meet the van tomorrow morning and shepherd them for the day, so I give him the student tickets and ours for tomorrow.

Steve, David, and I huddle together whispering our fears even though no noise could awaken Vic from his chemically induced coma. Suddenly alarms blare, and a doctor runs into the room, the same male nurse behind him. Vic's heart pounds impotently after having kept tempo for ten hours. *Can I bear this?* The nurse puts the paddles on Vic's chest.

"Stand back!"

Vic's body convulses. His heart resumes a normal rhythm.

Two panicked doctors have an animated discussion just outside the glass doors of Vic's room. David and I stand to meet them as they walk toward us.

"We have to transport him to Syracuse," they tell us. "We've ordered a Medevac helicopter."

"Take him to Strong Hospital in Rochester," I beg. "His oncologists are there. They know his situation. His case is too complex to start over with new doctors."

"Syracuse is closer. It's not safe to waste time." I feel powerless against their authority and expertise.

"May I ride with him?"

"Probably not, but it's up to the pilot. Ask him."

Two women nurses in pastel smocks tenderly slide Vic's inert body onto a wide stretcher covered with an unzipped body bag. I cradle Vic's feet in my hands while they transfer his IV lines and tubes to portable machines, taping loose wires to his body and settling pieces of equipment next to him. Finally, they switch the wires to a portable defibrillator and tuck it next to his belly. What can I do for him? I remember a small laminated photo of Anthony Damiani I carry in my wallet.

"May I put this photo on his chest?" I ask.

"Of course. We'll tape it over his heart so it won't get lost."

After placing the photo and double-checking the wires, the nurses cross Vic's hands over his chest, wrap him like a mummy, and zip the bag. They wheel him outdoors into the glaring October sun and slide him into the belly of a helicopter painted kindergarten primary colors. I climb in and put my hand on Vic's head, waiting to ask if I can ride along. My heart pounds, fearing the pilot will say no. David and a few friends stand outside the helicopter door, waiting.

Instead of preparing for takeoff, the pilot and doctors have an animated discussion on the helicopter pad. They repeatedly point to the screen of the pilot's handheld computer. I ask a friend to stay with Vic while David and I see what's happening.

"Is there a problem?" I ask the group of white-coated and uniformed men.

"I can't fly to Rochester," the pilot says apologetically. "A nasty line of thunderstorms has developed between here and there. We'll have to take him to Syracuse."

"No. Rochester," I insist, even though it seems impossible.

"Syracuse," the head doctor demands, towering over me. "We can't mess around."

"Don't take him to Syracuse," I plead. "In Rochester, there is a chance they'll know what's going on."

"Syracuse," the doctor commands the pilot, scowling at me.

"Does the helicopter have all the equipment needed if his heart goes into fibrillation again?" I ask the pilot, turning my back on the doctors.

"Yes, all our emergency transport vehicles have that," he says.

"Does this hospital have equipment to handle fibrillation that you don't have?"

"Not really. But I have to tell you," he points to a fiery red line on the weather map on his computer screen, "it's dangerous to fly to Syracuse, too. Thunderstorms are popping up all over the place, moving east fast."

"What should we do?" I ask the pilot, who seems to have more sense at the moment than the rest of us.

"I say it's too dangerous to fly. He should go in an ambulance."

"OK," I straighten my back and command the exasperated group of white-coated men gathered around me. "Order an ambulance and take him to Rochester."

"It's faster to take him to Syracuse," the doctor argues, as though I'm trying to kill my husband with my insistence. I see a cartoon bubble over his head that reads: "This woman is a hysterical obstinate maniac." He's wrong. I am a lioness protecting her cub.

"I take full responsibility for this decision," I tell him, looking him straight in the eye. "What difference does an extra half hour make? I understand you don't know what to do, but they won't know what to do in Syracuse either. Most doctors have never heard of the lymphoma he has. Call Rochester and tell them we're coming."

The doctor glares at me with weary resentful eyes, but acquiesces. Within minutes, the ambulance arrives and Vic's body is transferred from the helicopter.

"May I ride with you?" I ask the young driver. I am desperate to stay with Vic, to protect him and be with him if he dies on the way.

"Climb in the passenger seat and belt up. We'll be moving fast," he warns.

Behind me, Vic lies in his mummy suit with monitors and bags hanging from the ceiling, an EMT on each side. I can't touch him, but I can see him.

"We can handle this," the EMT tells me when I ask about her equipment, wanting reassurance, needing to make sure I've made the right decision.

The alert sweet-faced driver skillfully races through heavy rain, switching from one lane to another, sometimes sounding sirens and flashing lights, sometimes not. I appreciate his youthful testosterone. I'm grateful for this wild ride and grateful Vic's heart is beating. *Om Mani Padme Hum.*

In just over an hour, we pull up to the hospital emergency room entrance in Rochester. As they wheel Vic in, I glance up at the big letters over the doorway. STRONG. I exhale, knowing Vic is in the only place that might save him.

❧ ☙

The ER staff hustles the stretcher carrying Vic's body through swinging glass doors and whisks him away. They direct me to a small barren waiting room where the cardiologist will meet with me later. I am alone, bewildered, and wrung out, wishing I could wake up from this surreal nightmare. I try to follow my breath and feel the soles of my feet on the floor, remembering that my feet can find their way in the dark, even if my mind is lost.

I quiet myself enough to practice the Medicine Buddha meditation for Vic. As my diaphragm yields, I drop from a high red alert to a softer yellow anxiety. I got Vic here, but his destiny is not in my hands. I begin writing in the journal I take everywhere, the one that contains information about Vic's health and my reflections about our experience. I write an outline of the events from the last two days, compelled to remember every detail.

"He's doing well," the cardiologist tells me a few hours later, sitting close to me on the hard couch, his knees almost touching mine. His face is open, gentle, and relaxed, as though he has time to talk. "There have been no more incidents. We did a battery of tests and found no blockage or heart damage. His heart is pumping normally with good volume."

"When can I see him?"

"He's being wheeled upstairs to cardiac intensive care."

"What happened?" I ask. The doctor shrugs his shoulder and shakes his head from side to side, a gesture that has become all too familiar.

"I have no explanation. He has fluid buildup in his tissues, but not in his lungs or around his heart. Tomorrow morning, we'll get him off life support and see how he does. Then we'll try to figure out what happened so we can prevent it from happening again. I'm sorry I can't tell you more." He pats my shoulder with fatherly concern.

In cardiac intensive care, Vic's limp body lies on a white narrow elevated bed in another high-tech plastic and stainless-steel room. The nurse inspecting Vic's tubes and lines looks up and smiles as I enter the room.

"My name is Hamil," the brown-skinned nurse says in a soft voice with a Middle Eastern accent. "You must be Mr. Mansfield's wife. I will clean up your husband and redo some of the lines that were done in a hurry."

I stand close to Vic, touching and kissing his warm hand, whispering my love in his ear. Hamil works silently and slowly, gently removing the sloppy tape that secures the tubing and expertly sliding his hospital gown out from under him. She doesn't remove the photo of Anthony Damiani that's taped over Vic's heart. After redoing the IV lines, Hamil bathes Vic's body with warm water, touching him with the gentle compassion she might offer her child. The bath is a sacred ritual of baptism.

Thank you, Hamil. Thank you, Hamil. Thank you Divine Mother for the healing care of this kind woman, your handmaiden Hamil.

When Hamil has washed every part of Vic, she puts a clean gown over his body and enfolds him in white cotton blankets. Then she turns to me.

"What do you need?" she asks.

"May I sleep in this room?" I ask.

"Yes, yes, of course." She leaves and quickly returns pushing a reclining chair stacked with pillows and blankets. "The blankets are warm," she says as she hands me a bottle of water.

In a few hours, David arrives with a duffle bag of clothing he gathered for me at home. He buys me a sandwich from the hospital café and tucks me in before leaving to pick up Anthony at the airport. At one a.m., Anthony awakens me with a hug.

"Hi Momma," he whispers. Then he stands back from the bed, takes in the scene, and weeps. We all weep. We planned to see the Dalai Lama together today, but we are experiencing another kind of spiritual initiation.

I wake up at around four that morning and do the Medicine Buddha meditation, accompanied by the whooshing of the ventilator. I visualize the Dalai Lama pouring bowls of blue water over Vic's body, filling him with life.

As the hospital begins to stir, Dr. Fisher and Dr. Friedberg show up. Dr. Friedberg hugs me.

"Poor thing," he murmurs as he looks at Vic. "Poor thing."

"Spongy," Fisher says to Friedberg as he pokes at the lymph nodes under Vic's arm. "It doesn't feel like lymphoma. More like an infection or allergy."

May it be so, I pray.

Dr. Friedberg probes Vic's neck, underarms, and groin and orders a skin biopsy. I've seen his wrinkled brow before and know he's worried. When a new dermatologist arrives a few hours later, he can't find a rash. The cortisone cream has suppressed the rash so completely that there is still nothing to biopsy.

By the time David and Anthony arrive, the nurses have withdrawn Vic's drugs and he stirs. David is in constant motion bringing us food and water and making phone calls, while Anthony stands quietly against a wall, holding his grief close and inward. A nurse tells me that Vic will have amnesia and memory problems for several weeks.

His eyes still closed, Vic reaches up to pull the intubation tube from his throat. The nurse ties his hands to the bars of the bed, and he flails weakly, grabbing at tubes, trying to sit up. I hold one hand and David holds the other. We talk to him, trying to soothe him. By now it's midmorning and the Dalai Lama is leading an interfaith service in Ithaca.

"Do you want to see the Dalai Lama?" David asks his dad.

Vic nods yes. David puts Vic's laptop on the tray table, tips the screen toward Vic's face, and finds the livestream of the event. The three of us stand around Vic and watch the service we had planned to attend. Tears drip from his eyes when he sees the Dalai Lama, and then he falls asleep. *My poor dear one, so wounded, so beaten.*

When Vic wakes again, he squeezes my hand and tries to speak despite the tube down his throat. His eyes are urgent.

"Give him something to write on," a nurse suggests. I hold my notebook for him, untie his right hand, and put a pen in it. He scribbles a little, and then, like a first-grader learning his letters, he focuses on his task and slowly, with great effort, scrawls words on the page, tears pooling in the corners of his eyes.

"I am deeply appreciative for all help, love, and kindness. You people are Bodhisattvas. How did it start?" I can barely read his writing, but I read the words aloud and he nods yes when I get it right.

"You people are very kind. I love you. It heals!"

Around noon, the nurse pulls the tube from Vic's throat.

"What happened?" he whispers. I give him the short version—again and again. Like someone with dementia, he repeats his question, but I don't care. Vic is back. He can speak, and even if he doesn't quite get who I am, he knows he loves me.

"What's his name?" Vic asks when Anthony leaves for a moment. Later, when David steps out of the room, he says, "I forgot Anthony's name. And who is that other one?" By the end of the day, Vic has more memory. He loves everyone, a miraculous open-hearted worshipful love, despite what he's been through, perhaps because of what he's been through. Mostly he sleeps, but when he's awake he whispers words of sweet gratitude.

A few days later, the crisis is passed, although there are still no explanations. David drives Anthony to the airport and leaves for North Carolina. I hope Vic and I will go home in the next few days, but Vic has an erratic heartbeat, continued swelling, coughing, and buckets of mucus, although still no rash. Dr. Friedberg looks more concerned every day.

Then Vic's fever spikes to 104, putting him into jaw-rattling rigors and the nurses into panic. During rounds, the cardiologist shrugs his shoulders for the second time.

"He threw me another curve ball with this fever," the doctor says. "I'm baffled." They put Vic back on antibiotics. Infectious disease doctors hover around asking me questions about where Vic has traveled, looking for a mysterious infection. Friends visit from Ithaca with love and soup. We wait for the rash to return, still hoping it will prove that this is a drug reaction, not cancer.

The dermatologist tells us that a reaction to sulfa drugs can go on for weeks or months, but the cardiologist says a drug reaction should be over by now. He has no idea what's happening, but suggests an internal defibrillator in case it happens again. Dr. Friedberg says the blood work is inconclusive, so he wants a skin biopsy. Finally, ten days after the cardiac arrests, the rash returns.

The day after the biopsy, Vic gets the news while I'm outside walking in Mount Hope Cemetery.

"Friedberg was right," Vic reports in a quiet, sorrowful voice. "The rash, the swelling, the coughing, the exhaustion, the fever—all weird symptoms of lymphoma." Perhaps lymphoma in the lymph nodes around the heart caused the cardiac arrests, but there is no way to know for sure.

My face flushes and my jaws clench. I don't want to live with Vic's cancer, and I don't want him to die. I don't want to give my life to this chaos. I want to save my own ass, since I can't save his. I want to scream and cry, but there he is so pale and calm. Not trusting myself to speak, I rub his dry feet with skin cream and fight my impulse to run. I massage his fluid-filled legs, now swollen to twice their normal size. I don't want to care this much about his suffering. I don't want to love him this much. I don't want to need him this much. Even though it's not my body in the bed, his suffering ravages every part of me and my life. I saw what he didn't see when he was unconscious or drugged or delirious. I am his witness, and I am drowning.

"I have to go back to my hotel," I say with guilt and remorse, knowing he can read my reaction. I call Gita and Lourdes Brache-Tabar from my room, knowing these two friends will hold the anguish with me and understand my response. In a few hours, I'm calm enough to feel compassion for Vic and for myself.

"I love you, Vic," I tell him on the phone. "I love you and I'm sorry."

Now that the diagnosis is clear, Friedberg orders high doses of prednisone to ease Vic's symptoms and get him on his feet. Within an hour of taking the magic pills, Vic begins peeing out the fluid. The next day a defibrillator is inserted in his chest, and the day after that, an orderly wheels Vic to the front of the hospital while I get the car. All I want is home.

      ❦ ❧

A few weeks later, Lauren tells us that she saw the Dalai Lama the morning after Vic's cardiac arrests. Since there were only a few people in the room, she told the Dalai Lama about Vic's situation. His Holiness listened quietly as she explained what had happened and then he bowed his head and walked away. Before reaching the doorway, he turned back to Lauren.

"Everyone has to die sometime," he said, throwing his hands up in the air and releasing a cosmic, deep belly laugh.

"That's the Lion roaring in the face of death—unafraid," Vic says when Lauren tells him the story.

That winter, Vic is tortured with the trials of Job. He stops taking prednisone to try the experimental chemotherapy drugs that Dr. Friedberg suggests, but each time he goes off steroids, the worst symptoms return. Vic is immobilized by swelling and the fevers are terrifying, but he endures hoping that one of the chemo drugs will help. All he gets from the experimental drugs are mouth sores and more misery.

"You can't go on like this, Vic," I tell him.

I'm exhausted with watching this torture. It's obvious that the experimental drugs aren't helping and we know prednisone can help, at least temporarily. We have another conference with Michael Eisman who agrees there is no point to the suffering. Vic needs to accept any relief he can get.

"I can't do this anymore," Vic tells Dr. Friedberg on New Year's Eve. "Give me prednisone."

Within days, the swelling begins to disappear. Vic is a thin shell of who he was before, but he gradually gains strength. I write in my journal:

Dear Medicine Buddha,

I am trying. Vic is trying. Janet is trying. Michael is trying. Dr. Friedberg is trying. We all keep trying, but without YOU, there is no hope. If you need Vic's service and his work on your behalf, you'll have to help. He needs new energy, a drug that works, or a miracle. If you need Vic's service, help him. And if you do not need Vic to live, be merciful, be decisive, be fast.

∽ ∾

I dreamed I held an emaciated large-eyed young girl against the bare skin of my belly. The baby is a child of famine and I have to warm and protect her.

Recently I've had a series of upsetting dreams, but this starving girl startles me into finding psychological support. I make an appointment with Barbara Platek, a Jungian therapist in Ithaca, and set up a series of two-hour sessions every other week. It takes a full hour to tell my stories and weep. We devote the second hour to dreams where Barbara helps me find patterns that bring meaning to the mess of my life. I still feel battered, but also feel that I'm being held and guided through an initiation.

> But life holds mystery for us yet. In a hundred places
> we can still sense the source: a play of pure powers
> that—when you feel it—brings you to your knees.7

∽ ∾

With prednisone, Vic gains enough time to welcome his new book and go on the two-month tour he had scheduled the previous summer. I pack his suitcase and medicine and drive him to the airport for two- or three-day trips to universities where, between lectures, he rests in a hotel room. He moves forward with his warrior will, exhausted but inspired by each trip. Between short tours, he gathers his waning strength while I repack his clothes and medicines. Then he boards another plane.

When Vic is away, we talk on the phone and send many emails each day. I look forward to his loving email messages that come without the sound of coughing and the immediacy of his suffering. I can almost forget he's dying. On his last book trip to University of Missouri, he sends this message.

Dear Love,

I feel my love going out over the land, past Sandalia, the Little Dixie Game Reserve, on east to the Finger Lakes, and into Hector. Everywhere I look, I see the care and precision of your packing. Each little item thought out and put in the right place. It just shouts love at me. Deep thanks to you.

It was a lot of work getting here, but it gives me a chance to spread a little good around rather than just wait at home for the Grim Reaper. I continue to beam my love your way.

Vic

4

Grace heals. Hope sputters.
Love sustains.

By the end of Vic's book tour in April, his main source of calories is Ricola cough drops. Prednisone no longer suppresses his swelling and coughing; nothing works better. Each morning, he has a hangover from the high doses of Ambien and codeine he took the night before. After forcing down a few spoons of oatmeal, he takes large doses of prednisone with a pot of coffee. Somehow he stays on his feet, motivated by his desire to see the Dalai Lama one last time.

In 2006, Vic and another faculty member recommended Colgate invite the Dalai Lama to speak at the annual Global Leaders Lecture Series. The lecture and a two-day campus visit were scheduled for the spring of 2009; but in January of 2008, Colgate learned a space had opened in the Dalai Lama's schedule. Could Colgate host the Dalai Lama in April of 2008, just two and a half months away? Some brave soul said yes.

Tibetan Buddhism and Modern Physics would be published by then and, if Vic is still alive, he could present his book to the Dalai Lama in person. In March, we learn Vic and the Dalai Lama will speak at a

Buddhism and Science Colloquium on April 23. My goal is to keep Vic glued together until that day.

On April 22, the first day of the Dalai Lama's visit, Vic is excited like a schoolboy. He beams when he returns from the opening luncheon where he is seated directly across from the Big Guy. He beams throughout the afternoon public lecture, squeezing my hand with happiness and reaching out to caress his sons' shoulders. After a newspaper interview in the afternoon, Vic is spent. David, Anthony, and I help him to our hotel room and prepare a plate of food brought from home. Vic eats a few bites. His body convulses with coughing all night. Neither of us sleeps.

In the morning, Vic and I are the first two people in the eighty-seat lecture hall where the Buddhism and Science Colloquium will take place. I make sure Vic has enough cough drops and water. I slip him an extra codeine pill timed to take effect at ten a.m. when the discussion begins, draw a diagram on the blackboard that Vic needs for his talk, and save seats for David and Anthony. I pace. Finally, I sit down and surrender to exhaustion and relief. Despite all odds, Vic is here for this day.

Colgate's president Rebecca Chopp introduces the panel members and welcomes His Holiness. Then she nods to Vic, who walks toward the Dalai Lama holding out a silk-wrapped copy of his book and bows deeply. The Dalai Lama steps off the podium, moves close to Vic, and peers intently into his eyes. His voice breaking with tears, Vic thanks His Holiness for the spiritual, political, and intellectual inspiration he has given him, his students, and the world. The Dalai Lama grasps the book in his left hand and opens his arms like a mother reaching out for her suffering child. He cups the back of Vic's head with his right hand and pulls Vic into his maroon-clad shoulder. Vic gasps and sobs. Everyone in the room weeps with him.

"Well, we'll see if I can recover from that," Vic says with a sideward glance toward the audience and a shy smile. He wipes his tears with his shirt sleeve, takes a deep breath, pops a Ricola, and gives a fifteen-minute lecture on causality in physics that everyone in the room—scientists and nonscientists—can understand. He pauses frequently to give the translator time and make sure the Dalai Lama understands what he is saying. He ends his talk with a question for His Holiness about how causality in quantum mechanics relates to Buddhist causality.

I am achingly proud, proud to be Vic's wife, proud that he is here because of his will to complete his work, his good karma, and my unwavering care. Vic is a dying man, and after that hug, I sense his death close by.

Three other professors deliver talks from somewhere in the intellectual stratosphere. They speak so fast that the Dalai Lama's translator can't keep up, so His Holiness sits cross-legged on his throne-sized chair and leafs through Vic's book. When it is his turn to speak, the Dalai Lama makes a few general remarks. Then he turns toward Vic and answers the question about causality in Buddhism, in detail.

∾ ∾

After that embrace, Vic no longer fears his coming death. Sitting upright in his sickbed at home, he repeatedly watches the DVD of the Dalai Lama answering his question. Vic's mind is dulled by symptom suppressing drugs and the Dalai Lama's explanation of causality in Tibetan Buddhism is subtle, but finally Vic gets it. He keeps watching the video anyway.

Colgate sends Vic two photos, one of Vic offering his book to the Dalai Lama and one of the embrace, two men cheek-to-cheek, their faces buried in each other's shoulders. Vic carries the pictures back and forth between his desk and his bed and looks at them constantly. It assures him that the Dalai Lama's blessing is more than a dream. It is the sacred exclamation point to Vic's life.

∾ ∾

"Hope" is the thing with feathers –
That perches in the soul –
And sings the tune without the words –
And never stops – at all – [8]

By May the steroid-fueled respite that began four months ago is over. Prednisone held back the coughing and swelling longer than Vic's oncologist thought possible, but everyone knew it was a temporary fix.

Vic suggests we have a fortieth anniversary celebration on May 18. Throwing a party is the last thing I'm interested in doing, but as Vic's health worsens, I hire a caterer and invite friends for an evening of music and flowers, decadent food and love poetry. I do it for him—and to honor our marriage.

A year ago, four months after Vic's stem cell transplant, we celebrated our thirty-ninth anniversary, keenly aware there might not be another. We invited five couples with enduring marriages for dinner and asked them to bring something to read about love. We sat on the deck at sunset, drank red wine, and read aloud to one another. Vic and I read a poem we had read at our wedding in 1968.

. . . I need love more than ever now . . . I need your love,
I need love more than hope or money, wisdom or a drink

Because slow negative death withers the world – and only yes
Can turn the tide
Because love has your face and body . . . and your hands
     are tender
And your mouth is sweet – and God has made no other eyes
     like yours.[9]

It will be worth the effort to have a chance to read these lines to Vic again.

As our anniversary approaches, Vic grows weaker. By the end of each day, I grit my teeth against the barking cough and long to escape to my upstairs bedroom. For him, there is no escape.

Three days before the party, Dr. Friedberg suggests a chest X-ray. Michael Eisman is out of town, so we visit Vic's cardiologist Steven Goldberg. The X-ray shows scattered white spots on Vic's lungs.

"This looks like pneumonia, not cancer," Dr. Goldberg says, sounding sure. "I'll call Friedberg so he can admit you to the hospital in Rochester."

We know that even if it is pneumonia this time, cancer will never leave Vic alone. Still, pneumonia might be treatable, even though Vic's lungs have not responded to the powerful antibiotics he's been taking for weeks. No matter. Pneumonia sounds better than cancer, so we cling to the possibility.

I drive home from the cardiologist's office along the valley road between Corning and Watkins Glen. Spring-green hillsides shout out vitality and promise, while Vic coughs and gasps in the passenger seat next to me. Reminding myself to breathe, I use my cell phone to ask a friend to pick up Daisy and water the flats of plants I'm hardening off for the garden. I call the American Cancer Society Lodge in Rochester to reserve a room and make a mental list of what we need for what I pray will be a short hospital stay—photo of the Dalai Lama hugging Vic, laptop, pajamas for Vic, clothing for me, Vic's medicine, my vitamins, toothbrushes.

Vic slowly makes his way from the car to the house, leaning heavily into a cane. Between coughing jags, he packs his computer bag and gathers toiletries. I tear up and down the stairs with as much efficiency as I can muster. Needing to think straight and calm myself for the two-hour drive to Rochester, I steal a few seconds to pause at my bedroom window and look out at my avian neighbors in their nesting boxes who are incubating eggs.

After packing the car and getting Vic settled, I go back inside for a final house-check, straighten the sheets of Vic's hospital bed, and pick up a few sets of earplugs to protect Vic from hospital noise. I look around

Vic's office, check to make sure he's packed his reading glasses, and pause for a long last look through the telescope that focuses not on the distant hills or on the moons of Jupiter, but on the round doorway of a bluebird box.

A male bluebird sits on the roof, his blue back shimmering in the afternoon sun. A rusty orange patch of chest feathers arches triumphantly over his white belly as he twists on his perch to scan the territory and guard his mate and their eggs.

The bluebird who claimed the house this year may not be the same as the one who nested there last year. Last year's king may have died or been deposed by his offspring. Death takes what it will take and ends what it must end, but alongside constant loss and destruction stands the solace of life's exuberant cycles. For a moment, I feel a quiet comfort, a faith that all is as it should be and that life is strong and sure even when death wins a local battle.

That night, Dr. Friedberg tells us Vic will be in the hospital for at least a few days. I email our friends and cancel the anniversary party.

∞ ∞

The next morning, Dr. Friedberg orders the pulmonary department to drain the fluid around Vic's lungs to make him more comfortable. I can't imagine another invasive procedure, but even without sleep or food Vic's will to live remains unbroken. He longs to take a deep breath.

That evening, a red-faced white-coated pulmonologist and his tense students surround Vic's bed.

"You sit on the side of the bed and lean forward on that tray table so we can work on your back," the pulmonologist orders Vic. "You stand in front of him. Push on the table and let him lean into you so that nothing moves," he orders me, polluting the air with irritability. Someone added this procedure to the end of this man's long day and he will punish all of us for the inconvenience. His students are tense and cautious as they follow his brusque directions, sterilize Vic's back, and insert a needle into the fluid-filled space around Vic's lungs. Unable to speed the suctioning process, the doctor paces behind Vic's bed, his resentment simmering just under the surface. Vic looks up at me with exhausted, sad eyes. I want to vaporize this doctor.

"Will you read the poem about kindness?" Vic asks in a whisper.

"Now?" I ask.

"Yes, now. Please." I think he's lost his mind but ask one of the students to hold Vic steady for a moment. I get Vic's book *Tibetan Buddhism and Modern Physics* from his briefcase and take my position again. Despite the strange sucking sounds, a smell of fetid saltwater, a horrifying amount of cloudy fluid dripping into plastic containers, and my embarrassment, I read the poem that ends Vic's book:

> Before you know what kindness really is
> you must lose things,
> feel the future dissolve in a moment
> like salt in a weakened broth.
> What you held in your hand
> what you counted and carefully saved,
> all this must go so you know
> how desolate the landscape can be
> between the regions of kindness.
> How you ride and ride
> thinking the bus will never stop,
> the passengers eating maize and chicken
> will stare out the window forever.
> Before you learn the tender gravity of kindness,
> you must travel where the Indian in a white poncho
> lies dead by the side of the road. . . .

The pulmonologist's jaw loosens and his hard voice softens. The students sigh and touch Vic's back with tenderness. My belly loosens and Vic takes a deep breath. Twilight dissolves the hard stainless edges of the equipment and a humming grace descends over the room.

You must see how this could be you,
how he too was someone
who journeyed through the night with plans
and the simple breath that kept him alive.
Before you know kindness as the deepest thing inside,
you must know sorrow as the other deepest thing.
You must wake up with sorrow.
You must speak to it till your voice
catches the thread of all sorrows
and you see the size of the cloth.
Then it is only kindness that makes sense anymore,
only kindness that ties your shoes
and sends you out into the day to mail letters
     and purchase bread,
only kindness that raises its head
from the crowd of the world to say
It is I you have been looking for,
and then goes with you everywhere
like a shadow or a friend.[10]

Once again, I ponder the wisdom of the Dalai Lama's core teaching. It matters not if we are Buddhists or Hindus, Jews or Christians, Muslims or Animists. What matters is that we invite light into the darkness of our fellow sufferers and heal the world with kindness.

"Kindness," the Dalai Lama says, "is my religion."

It is my religion, too.

The next morning, our anniversary, Vic looks and feels stronger. To celebrate, I buy him a soy cappuccino from the gourmet coffee shop in the hospital lobby. While he sips his coffee, I check my email. There is a message from Vic with the subject line: Happiest May 18 I could imagine.

My dearest love Elaine,

Without doubt, you have brought me more joy than any single thing in my life. I am sorry it is not better now, but I have hopes that it soon will be.

With much love, Vic

Celebrating our anniversary in a hospital room, I remember my favorite wedding photo from May 18, 1968. Vic has a thick red-tinged beard and black wavy hair. I'm wearing a pale yellow mini-dress I made for the day. My head rests on Vic's left shoulder and my neck arches back to receive his kiss on the bridge of my nose. My body asks him to protect me. His body says, I will.

∽ ≈

A few days later, Vic breathes freely. After he is injected with a new experimental chemotherapy drug, I transport him to the car in a wheel-chair and drive him home. I long to check on the bluebirds, walk the trails with Daisy, and plant lettuce. Despite my better judgment, hope floats in, ethereal and transient as a feather.

∽ ≈

"I can't imagine living here without you," I tell Vic. It's nearly a week since he came home from the hospital. Walking the trails a few times a day soothes me, but the grasses are higher than my boot tops and need to be mowed. We have tended this property together since 1972, and the challenge of caring for it on my own begins to sink in.

"Do what is right for you, E. You'll know what to do." Of course, the decision is in my hands. We both know that Vic won't be part of my future.

A few hours ago, Vic ventured outside and walked around the yard for a few minutes, but now he's sitting at his computer reading the *New York Times.*

"I'm afraid to use the bush hog, Vic. I hate to ask, but I need another lesson."

"OK, E. Let's do it."

He slowly pulls on his overalls and grabs a hat to protect his fragile skin from the May sun. As we walk down hill to the barn, he leans into a cane, breathing heavily even though we move at a snail's pace. I feel like a jerk asking him for anything, but I am cornered and panicked.

In the barn, I jump up on the Kubota and try to look confident. Vic stands next to the tractor, pointing and coughing.

"First turn the key halfway and wait for the amber glow plug light to go off," he instructs in his weakened raspy voice. "Make sure the gear shift is in neutral and the emergency brake is on. Step on the clutch and turn on the ignition. It's just like the car."

He tried to teach me to drive the tractor many times, but I was an unwilling student and he gave up. The tractor is a big, orange, die-sel-belching monster. It doesn't feel one bit like our Subaru to me.

After the engine roars to a start, Vic raises his voice, punctuating his sentences with fiercer bouts of coughing.

"Don't be in a hurry. Let it warm up." Then he reviews the mechanics of the bush hog. "Keep the rotary blade lifted and disengaged until you want to mow. In the rough spots, watch out for tree stumps. You'll be OK."

I haltingly drive the tractor to the south side of the barnyard, pull on the emergency brake, and run to the house to get my wide-brimmed hat. Inside, I glance out the window and see Vic hoist himself up on the tractor seat with a Herculean effort.

"Stop," I yell as I run outside, waving my hat to get his attention. "I can do it."

As I round the corner of the house he drives away, drops the bush hog blade to the grass, and begins cutting the trail just beyond the barn. A wave of shame burns my cheeks, even though I'm glad to escape the tractor one more time.

5

Waiting for death. What about me?

On May 27, at three a.m., the cell phone rings from the table next to my bed, startling me from a restless sleep. The call is from Vic, as I knew it would be. Too weak to climb the stairs, he calls my cell phone when he needs me. He's downstairs trying to make it through the night by sitting upright in his hospital bed. We have an appointment with Dr. Friedberg today, I remember, but we don't have to wake up this early. I want to sleep.

"I'm sorry, E. I can't breathe. I have to go to the hospital now." His voice is raspy and weak.

"OK, Love. I'll be right down."

I stifle my irritation. I know my impatience comes from exhaustion. I also know that if Vic says he can't wait a few more hours to see the doctor then he is desperate. He is stoic about his discomfort, but inability to breathe produces a physical panic that's hard to overcome. Adrenaline surges through my body and sends me into action.

"Should I call an ambulance?" I ask Vic as I sit close to him holding his hand.

"I don't know," he whispers with a weak shrug of his shoulders.

I take that to mean that there is a little space here and that I have time to figure out what to do. I call Strong Hospital and talk to the oncology resident on duty who tells me to call an ambulance and get Vic to an emergency room immediately. Since it's nearly a two hour drive to Rochester, this is what I expected her to say, but I've been through this before. In local emergency rooms, doctors don't know what to do. At best, after Vic spends the night on a hard cold pallet, they send him home in the morning and advise him to see his oncologist or cardiologist as soon as possible. At worst, he has a crisis they manage poorly. I don't blame them. His cancer and heart complications are incomprehensible even to the doctors who have treated him for two years.

I sit quietly next to Vic for a moment, looking him over. His body is red and swollen as it has been for months. His breath is labored and fast, but I've heard it worse. He leans into me as I hold his hand and take his pulse. His heart pounds, but it's not erratic as it sometimes is. With me at his side, his breathing eases a little.

"I think I should drive you to Rochester," I suggest. "If your breathing gets worse on the way, there are hospitals in Geneva and Canandaigua."

"I don't know what to do," Vic mutters.

It's up to me.

I drive through a misty dawn toward the emergency room in Rochester with one eye on the road and the other eye on Vic. His breath stays shallow and fast, but constant. At the ER entrance, I again notice the word STRONG over the door, only this time the message is for me rather than for Vic.

❖ ❖

I wait until eight a.m. to call North Carolina.

"Your dad's in the hospital again," I tell David with the calmest voice I can muster. "I drove him to Rochester before dawn."

"Oh, God. I'm sorry, Mom. How is he now?"

"Oxygen calmed him down. He's sitting upright on a narrow hard bed in the ER, waiting for a room in the oncology unit. He's restless, cold, and exhausted, but not in crisis."

"How are you, Mom?" David can hear the tears in my voice. I turn away from Vic, hoping he won't catch my words.

"I'm empty, David. A few minutes ago, I said to your dad, 'There is no comfort possible in your body, Vic. I want to help you, but I don't know how, so please don't tell me how much your back hurts until we get you into a regular room.'"

It shames me that I said this to the person I love most in this world, but it's a relief to confess. I know David won't judge me as harshly as I judge myself. Exhaustion and despair grind down the generosity of the heart. Usually I cringe at nothing, but my animal body senses that Vic is a lost cause.

What about me? My voice howls piteously inside my head. *What about me?*

"I'm getting a plane ticket, Mom. I'll be there later today."

"No, no. You can't do that," I protest. "What about your trip to Slovakia?"

"Today is Tuesday, Mom. I'm not leaving until Thursday morning."

"He shouldn't try to come here," Vic whispers breathlessly, catching the drift of the conversation. "They'll drain my lungs again. I'll be OK," he gasps. "He's been planning this trip for months. He should go."

"Don't come, David," I say. "It's too hard. We'll be OK."

"I'm hanging up, Mom. I'll call as soon as I know the plane schedule."

I meet David at the airport in the late afternoon. He is solid, strong, and ruddy with life. I sink into his familiar arms. *How could I have resisted this?*

The sun sets as we enter the hospital. Vic sits with his feet dangling over the edge of the bed, pale and woozy, struggling to stay upright. With David here, my heart opens to Vic's suffering once more. I stand in front of him, grasp his shoulders, and gently pull his weight toward me. His body presses into me, his right cheek against my chest. David sits on the bed behind his dad, stroking, massaging, ironing out the knots in Vic's back. In an hour, Vic relaxes a little and leans back into his pillows. Then he urges us to get some sleep.

David and I drive to Hope Lodge for the night where I reserved an extra room. Waiting to calm down so I can sleep, I remember a favorite family story.

∽ ≍

When Vic came home from work, four-year-old David waited for him by the front door.

"My feet hurt," Vic told little David. "They've been hurting all day, and I don't know what's wrong."

David looked worried.

"Oh, how my feet hurt," Vic moaned. "Do you see anything wrong with my feet?"

"Oh, Daddy," David exclaimed, his eyes bright with discovery. "You put your shoes on the wrong feet."

"That's silly. I wouldn't do that," Vic said looking down at his feet. Then he threw his hands up in mock alarm. "You're right, David. That's why they hurt. My shoes are on the wrong feet!"

Vic reached over to tickle David who let loose with the clear loud laugh of innocence.

"They're the fruit of the love tree," Vic said as he picked up one-year-old Anthony. The baby had no idea what was going on, but laughed at the joke anyway.

∽ ≍

At the hospital the next morning, Vic again sits upright, his legs hanging over the side of the bed. His eyes are half-closed, wet, and full of love.

"While you went to the airport yesterday, Dr. Friedberg told me they think cancer is causing the fluid in my lungs." He speaks slowly, pausing for air. "The full report came in from last week's skin biopsy. Now there are two kinds of lymphoma," Vic whispers. "Prednisone isn't holding it back. They'll drain my lungs again. They aren't optimistic. Friedberg suggests hospice or salvage chemotherapy."

Salvage chemotherapy—the end of the line possibility when nothing else works. And Vic knew last night that we had come to this junction.

"Why didn't you tell us yesterday?" I ask.

"I wanted you to sleep," Vic says, pausing for air between each sentence. "Friedberg promised he'd come back this morning to talk to you. I needed to think it through. I want to try the chemotherapy. It will give me a few good months, or it will make me die faster."

What about me? What about me?

Salvage chemotherapy means hospitalization for at least one out of every three weeks for months. It means terrible symptoms for Vic to endure after each treatment. It means that I have to be strong enough to witness more suffering. Even if he gets a few good months, Death will still hover. There is no escape.

"Go for it, Dad." David says while I wrestle with my feelings. David sounds sure. We call Anthony in California who plans to fly home in a few days. He's sure, too. The three guys agree, but I will be the one with Vic when David and Anthony go home to their lives.

Dr. Friedberg comes in to talk with us late in the morning. He wants to start the chemotherapy tonight.

"Let's do it," Vic says in a little voice that sounds unable to do anything at all.

"OK," I agree reluctantly.

I leave David and Vic in the hospital room and walk alone through the familiar roads of Mount Hope Cemetery, considering the precipice on which we stand. Hospice or salvage chemotherapy. I doubt I would make the same choice Vic is making, but I need to figure out if I have the guts to keep supporting his battle.

"Your dad's a warrior, not because he chooses to be, but because he can't help it," I tell David as I drive him to the airport late in the afternoon. "I knew he would take the steep path all the way to the end. He doesn't want to drag this out any longer. Neither do I. I can't stand watching him die, and I can't stand watching him live this way. Mostly I can't stand perching on this threshold any longer." I pause to wipe my tears and take a breath.

"It's OK, Mom," David reassures me. "I'm crying, too."

"David, they can't stop his dying, but maybe they will push the lymphoma back one more time. I'll get more help from friends. You and Anthony will come home often this summer. With your support, I say, 'Yes'."

It's decided. Chemotherapy begins tonight. David flies to Slovakia tomorrow after reassurance from Dr. Friedberg that Vic's death is likely months away. I will soldier on.

Driving back to the hospital, I consider the no-win trap I'm in. I want Vic's suffering to end, but I don't want him to die. If he continues to live, he will suffer, no matter how much I plead and pray. Part of me begs Death to come quickly. Salvage chemotherapy could make that happen. *Let his suffering end. Let me collapse, mourn, and get on with whatever life I have.* Then I circle back to the stark truth that ending Vic's suffering means ending Vic. He's been at my side since I was a girl. How will I handle the grief of losing him without him here to wipe my tears and hear my lament?

When I enter Vic's room, he waves me toward him and wraps his arms around me. We entwine like morning glory vines. Until we are forced apart, we are together.

Unbearable outcomes lie ahead, but today there are poems to read, soup to heat, and feet to rub. Am I strong enough to open to this moment and not wish for anything? Can I remember that I'm not alone in my suffering or my wish to avoid it? I pray for an inner quiet that will allow me to spend our last days together in peace. Then I turn to Vic, arrange his pillow, and caress his cheek.

At ten p.m., we still wait for the chemotherapy drugs. Once again, I long to escape. Vic sits on the side of the bed, bracing himself with his arms. I know my exhaustion is nothing compared to his.

"Please lie down, Vic," I beg.

"My back hurts," he murmurs.

I rub his back and try to help him find a better position. He looks up at me with huge liquid eyes.

"I am not afraid," he whispers with fierce conviction, looking at the photo of the Dalai Lama hugging him that I taped on the wall. "I am not afraid."

I feel myself pull back, step away from this gaping hole into the world of death. I have gone as deep as I can go.

"Will you meditate with me when the chemo comes?" he asks.

"Vic, I've been on high alert for days. I need to lie down. I have done the Medicine Buddha practice with you and for you for years. I will do it tonight in bed and in the morning, but I have to lie down. I'm sorry. I need strength to face tomorrow and then another tomorrow. I'll be back early in the morning."

I stand in front of him and gently draw his body toward mine, supporting his weight, trying to make up for my guilt at leaving him alone. My tears drip into his hair.

"Thank you, E, for everything," he whispers. "Thank you for loving me. I'm so sorry."

That night, I envision the Medicine Buddha's healing liquids before falling into a dreamless sleep.

At seven the next morning, Vic calls to tell me he's OK, whatever that means. We weep together on the phone. When I get to the hospital, clear chemo fluid drips into his arm. I ask him if he wants something to eat, even though he's hardly eaten for a month.

"Soy ice cream with a banana sounds good," he says.

What I don't know is that this is his last meal. I don't know that I will not do the Medicine Buddha practice with him again. I don't know that salvage chemotherapy will offer him the fastest way out. I don't know that, even though it cannot save him, chemotherapy will stop the cough that has racked his body for months and bring him the blessing of a quiet gentle death.

∽ ∾

"Shouldn't he get out of bed and move around?" I ask the nurse. This graying Vietnam vet with acne scars has cared for Vic during this hospital stay, gently patching bedsores and offering warm blankets and clear explanations.

"No, not now," he says. "He's too sick to get up."

"Is he dying? He's nearly comatose. This looks to me like dying."

"Salvage chemotherapy is like this for someone as sick as he is. Let him rest. But you might want to talk to the social worker. Her office is three doors down the hall."

"Can I hire someone to sit with my husband a few hours a day so I can get a break?" I ask the social worker.

"What about your friends? They've offered to help, haven't they?"

"They have," I say, "but they live two hours away."

"Let them help anyway," she advises, "and you should go home for a night." She's obviously seen a few burned-out spouses in her time. "When your husband goes home next week, he'll be sicker than he is now and you'll have to care for him alone. He'll need you more then, so why don't you take the night off while you can and let us take care of him?"

"How can he be sicker than this?" I ask.

"Salvage chemo is rough."

"Is he dying?" I ask the oncologist on duty.

"No, no. This is the usual response. He's exhausted. It's good that he's resting."

In desperation, I call Steve and ask him to come to the hospital and stay with Vic tonight and tomorrow morning.

"Yes, I'm glad to help," Steve says in his deep reassuring voice.

I call Barbara who volunteers to meet me tomorrow morning in my garden to plant and weed. I'll sleep in my own bed, work outside in the morning, and then drive back to the hospital.

"I need to go home tonight. Is that OK?" I ask Vic. He looks at me through blurry half-here eyes. "I'll be back tomorrow afternoon, but I need to rest tonight."

He nods yes, but I'm not sure he understands what I'm saying. I tug at the pale blue hospital gown that gaps open and exposes his bare back. Barely conscious, he sits on the edge of the bed and resists my attempt to push him back against the pillows. It's torture watching him fight to keep his balance.

I need to stop holding him up now, so I have strength to hold him up next week.

"I dreamed that the Spanish king is dead, but I don't know about it," Vic had told me yesterday morning. "I don't know what it means," he said in a halting voice. He was still curious about the offerings of his psyche. I considered the warning, but there had been many before.

Steve arrives around six that evening. He holds me close against his sinewy body before he sits on the bed and pushes his strong back up against Vic's for support. Leaving them back to back, I escape from the hospital and drive home.

⋙ ⋘

I drop my overnight bag by the front door, stick my cell phone in my pocket, and hurry out to the twilit garden, grabbing a narrow shovel on the way. I work up a sweat digging out thistle roots that have taken over the north end of the vegetable patch. They got their start last fall when Vic was in the hospital.

In the last rays of light, my cell phone rings. It's Steve's number. I hope he's calling to tell me that Vic is resting and doing better.

"I'm the resident on duty," a harried woman's voice says. "Your husband won't lie down. He's groggy and disoriented. I pushed back him into his pillows and he swore at me. Maybe he's had a stroke. I'm taking him for a CT scan, but don't know how I'll get him to lie down."

"Take Steve with you," I tell her. "Vic trusts Steve and will do what he asks. Should I drive back to Rochester now?"

"No, no. I'll call after the scan" the resident says. "We'll decide then."

She calls around eleven. "The scan showed nothing. He's still sitting up, but he seems stable."

"Should I come right now?"

"No, I'll call if there's any change. I'll call in the morning no matter what."

I put my cell phone next to my bed, take half of one of Vic's Ambien, and drop into an intermittent restless sleep. *I should be at the hospital, not home. I'm in the wrong place. Why did I leave?* I wait for the phone to ring. I get up a number of times intending to grab my bag and drive to Rochester, but then lie down again exhausted. I wake up at dawn. *Why hasn't the resident called? Why hasn't Steve called?* I realize that I don't have a phone number for the nurses' station. I didn't need a phone number when I was always there. *Why hadn't I thought of this?* I scold myself for the oversight. It takes a panicked half-hour to find the phone number, but I finally reach the nurses' station. A woman answers.

"My husband is there," I tell her. "Vic Mansfield. Can you tell me how he's doing?"

"Every doctor on the ward is in his room right now. That's not a good sign."

"Can I talk to one of them?"

"I'll have them call you."

I know how reliable that is, so I call Steve who is sleeping for a few hours at his friend's house near the hospital. I ask him to go to the hospital, call me from Vic's room, and tell me what's happening. Then I call Michael Eisman. No answer. I call the nurses' station again. The doctors are still in Vic's room. Yes, she'll tell them to call me.

I drive toward Rochester through the clearing light, thoughts and memories colliding into each other, praying for my breath and mind to slow down. The golden morning holds the promise of a beautiful day, a good day to live, a good day to die.

When I'm not dialing the cell phone, I repeat *Om Mani Padme Hum*, the mantra given to me first by Anthony Damiani and second by the

Dalai Lama. I still can't reach Michael. I call Barbara and tell her I can't plant this morning. *Om Mani Padme Hum.* She calls back to tell me she's coming to Rochester with Janet. I call Lauren. David has already left for Europe. I phone Anthony. It's five a.m. in California and he doesn't answer. I keep driving, controlling my speed with the cruise control, trying to keep my mind steady on the road while my heart pounds. *Om Mani Padme Hum.*

Steve calls. A new pulmonary doctor waits at his side to talk to me.

"His lungs filled again. He won't make it more than a few hours unless we put him on a respirator. What do you want to do?"

Now I understand why Vic wouldn't lie down yesterday. *Why didn't I see that? Why didn't the doctors understand that his lungs were full? What do I want to do? I want to wake up from this nightmare. Yesterday they said Vic was managing the chemotherapy fairly well, but now they say he's dying.*

"I need to talk to an oncologist," I tell the doctor. Dr. Friedberg flew to Europe the day after he ordered salvage chemotherapy, so I have to make a decision without him. I try Michael's number again and formulate my question for him and the oncologist.

"If you put Vic on a respirator, is it possible he will recover enough to receive more treatments and eventually get off the respirator?"

This is the only question that matters.

"No, I don't think he can tolerate more chemotherapy," the oncologist tells me when he calls. Just as I expected. *Om Mani Padme Hum.*

When I'm about an hour from the hospital, Michael calls. He spoke with the pulmonologist and oncologist before calling me and repeats the bad news.

"It's unlikely Vic will make it another hour without a respirator," Michael says gently. "If he's put on a respirator, he'll die within a few weeks, heavily drugged in intensive care." I trust his calm quiet voice and know he's telling me what the pulmonologist knew but dared not say.

"He might not live until you get there. Do you want them to put him on a respirator so you can be with him at the end?"

It's unbearable to be away from Vic at his death. I've been at his side for forty-two years of love and two have been years of illness. I made love with him and told him my secrets. I gave birth to our babies with him beside me. I held his hand during bone marrow biopsies, chemotherapy, and a stem cell transplant. I held him through a night of repeated cardiac arrest. But it's wrong to ask him to go through one more procedure for my sake. Maybe it's easier for him to slip out of his body without me holding his hand. Let Steve be the midwife for this passage. What do I know about the ways of life and death? I only know I can minimize the suffering now, perhaps for both of us.

"No respirator," I tell Michael. I call Steve's phone. "Tell the doctor, no respirator."

With that decision, the phone grows quiet. I drive down the Thruway alert, awake, broken-hearted, and oddly calm. I pray for an easy passage for Vic. *Om Mani Padme Hum.*

∽ ∾

The calm fades and my heart pounds as I park the car and hurry through the hospital corridors. Five doctors are in Vic's room. The bed is cranked to an upright position and Vic slumps against pillows with an oxygen mask on his face and machines on either side of him. He's alive. Steve paces at the foot of the bed.

"Do you still want to end treatment?" a doctor asks.

"Are you sure he won't be strong enough to get more chemotherapy?" I ask. I need to hear what I already know.

"Yes, quite sure."

"A respirator will only delay the inevitable?"

"Yes."

"Then stop."

Avoiding eye contact, the doctors unplug everything except the oxygen and IV pole, make a final check of the room, gather their equipment, and disappear like ghosts.

∞ ∞

Steve and I are alone with Vic and the familiar male nurse. In a stupor, Vic tugs at the large oxygen mask covering his face.

"He'll be more comfortable with the small nose dispenser he had before," the nurse says as he makes a fast switch from the mask to a nosepiece. Vic settles.

"Can I do anything else for you?" the nurse asks. He must be able to do something, but I don't know what.

A woman resident I've seen before comes into the room. She's dressed in street clothes. She whispers that she's not on duty, but heard from another doctor that Vic is dying. This resident spent hours with Vic during his last hospital stay, talking late into the night. Vic charms everyone from residents to orderlies. He asks them about their lives and talks straight about mortality and what he's learned about love and kindness. They tell him their troubles and fall in love with him—not for the advice he gives but for the questions he asks and his attention to their answers.

The resident is dark-skinned and lovely. Her unflinching eyes weep when Vic doesn't respond to her. When she hugs me, her tears dampen my shirt. Then she steps into her doctor's shoes.

"Begin a morphine drip," she tells the nurse. "Just 1 mg." I remember that Michael suggested morphine when I talked to him in the car, so I'm grateful. She asks if I would like hospice to come in and calls in the head nurse to discuss the options. Do I want to move Vic to the hospice wing of the hospital? Do I want to take him home in an ambulance? Do I want to stay where we are and have hospice come to us? I'm exhausted with decisions.

"Vic is peaceful now that you're here, Elaine," Steve tells me. Steve stands at the edge of Vic's bed. His words bring my attention to the stillness in the room now that the machines and doctors are gone.

Vic is propped upright with pillows at his sides and around his head.

When the resident and I adjust his pillows and move him just inches, he becomes agitated and gasps for air. He can't be moved without heavy morphine. I know Vic would rather have a conscious death than a drugged one and assume he doesn't care where he dies as long as I am with him. So I decide to stay in this small single room with a big window on the sky.

"Come as soon as you can," I tell Anthony when he calls from California. Steve sends emails and leaves word at the emergency phone number David left us. Barbara and Janet arrive, and then Lauren. I call Vic's mother and tell her that many of our friends have offered to drive her from Ithaca to the hospital in Rochester, but she decides not to come.

"God won't take my only son," she tells me. Nothing I say makes her change her mind.

I talk softly in Vic's ear. I tell him that he is dying, that there is nothing more the doctors can do, that I am with him and will walk with him to the edge. The nurse tells me that Vic is conscious, but too exhausted to move or speak. I don't ask him to communicate through hand squeezes or blinks. It feels wrong to call him back to life.

I have made the rational decisions and cleared the pathway to Vic's death. I'm stunned, exhausted, and heartbroken, but relieved to be at the end of this war. White flags of surrender. Death, enter this room and do what you will.

৶ ৵

Anthony calls in a few hours to say he can't get a plane until tomorrow morning. By then, Steve and Lauren have offered to stay with Vic and me to the end. I hadn't even asked. Other friends from Wisdom's Goldenrod arrive to say good-bye. Sometimes Vic opens his eyes a little, scans the room, and shuts them again. Friends take turns reading passages from *The Tibetan Book of Living and Dying*, Paul Brunton's books, and Rainer Maria Rilke's poetry. We meditate. We chant. *Om Mani Padme Hum*. We touch Vic—usually one person on each side of the bed, sometimes another at his feet. Lauren moistens his mouth. I caress his face and head, oil his feet, hold his hand, and inhale him. It's odd that death smells so sweet. By evening, the cancerous lumps on Vic's arms shrink and he stops coughing. Salvage chemotherapy kills the cancer cells even as he dies.

Vic labors over his breath. We wait.

෯ ෨

The next morning, Anthony's plane leaves California and David calls from Slovakia to say he can't get a flight for twenty-four hours. More friends show up to say good-bye, a few with food for those keeping vigil. I stay close to Vic.

During our second day of waiting, we read, chant, and tell stories about Vic, and soon a meditative quiet settles over the room. Late in the afternoon, Lauren and Barbara convince me to take a short walk in the cemetery. I don't want to leave, but friends are with Vic and will call if there is any change. I may have to step away for him to exit, so this is his chance. The intense blue sky, warm sun, and bursting green earth startle me, but as Rilke has taught me, each experience contains both life and death. After taking in life for twenty minutes, I hurry back to Vic's room.

He is the same when I return.

When Anthony calls, it's almost dark on this long June day. His plane circled Newark for more than two hours, but landed in Harrisburg because it was running out of gas. He's in a rented car heading north.

"Anthony will be here in three hours," I whisper to Vic, "but you don't have to wait." There is no sign that he hears me.

A few hours later Anthony calls from the New York border. Vic is only breath now. He works hard, like an experienced athlete moving toward the finish line. He goes long seconds without breathing, but then takes a huge gasp.

"He's getting lots of oxygen in those big breaths," the nurse tells me, "so this could go on a few more hours." We now hold vigil for Anthony's arrival and Vic's departure. Anthony calls when he's twenty miles from Rochester.

"Anthony will be here in half an hour," I whisper in Vic's ear. "You don't have to wait. Go when you need to go. We're here with you."

As Anthony drives into the parking garage, Steve talks to him on his cell phone and gives directions to the room. Barbara walks toward the elevator, meets Anthony in the hall, and walks him to Vic's bedside. Friends vacate the chairs. Anthony sits down, slides one hand under his dad's limp right hand, and wipes tears from his eyes with his other hand. I'm on the opposite side of the bed, at Vic's head.

"Anthony is here, Vic. Anthony is here," I whisper.

Vic who has been unresponsive with closed or vacant eyes for a day and a half opens his eyes wide and looks clearly and purposefully into Anthony's eyes. Their gaze meets in a sacred moment of transmission—a father taking leave of his son and passing along some mysterious blessing. Anthony continues to hold his father's hand as Vic's eyes close. It's close to midnight. Rhythmic, quiet, shallow breaths with long intervals between replace the gasping. We wait.

I hover around Anthony, sit in the chair next to him, and tell him he can move closer to his dad. Anthony focuses only on Vic, holding his hand and watching his face. I need to back away and let him say good-bye, so I lie on a pile of cotton blankets on the floor at the end of Vic's bed. Lauren promises to let me know if Vic's breathing changes. I struggle to hear his breath over the hospital fans as I drop into momentary darkness. *Om Mani Padme Hum.*

"His breathing changed," Lauren whispers in my ear. I jump to Vic's side. Anthony sits quietly, still holding his dad's hand. We wait, but there is no inhalation. He is gone. Slipped away while Anthony kept watch.

The last lines of the Heart Sutra pass through my mind: *Gone, gone, gone beyond, gone totally beyond. Oh, what an awakening!*

◈ ◈

Lauren and I lower the bed and tuck a single pillow under Vic's head so that, for the first time in many months, his body lies flat. We straighten his legs and cross his hands over his belly. I wipe his face, smooth his short dark hair, and walk to the nurses' station to ask them to turn off the morphine drip. It's past midnight and the hospital is dim and hushed.

Sometime after two, Lauren guides my hands to Vic's chest. Even though his hands and feet are cold, warmth emanates from his heart. I caress him and kiss his cool face, inhaling the scent of sweet damp earth. Anthony falls into an exhausted sleep on a couch in the waiting room across the hall, and Lauren and Steve collapse on piles of cotton hospital blankets on the floor. I curl up next to Vic's bed in an uncomfortable reclining chair, following my breath until my body slumps into unconsciousness.

It is still dark when I wake up. Was it all a dream? No, there he is, tranquil and handsome against the white sheets, the struggle over. Lauren hears my stirring, yawns, and waits while I shuffle down the darkened hallway to the nurses' station to ask for clean linens and a basin.

"Yes, yes, of course," an unfamiliar nurse says. "I'll get warm water, towels, and a clean gown." She also brings a body bag.

I wash and dry my lover's body, caressing his head and face, his limbs and belly, remembering the countless women before me who washed their dead. I tape the small photo of our teacher Anthony Damiani over Vic's heart, the same photo I taped on his chest after the cardiac arrests. Finally I look over at the body bag. It's plastic, crinkly, and heavily zippered.

"I'll take care of that after you leave," the nurse says quietly.

"No, I want to do it," I tell her. "May I have more clean sheets?" At least I can shield Vic's skin from the plastic.

I swaddle Vic's body in white cotton, cover his face, and carefully tuck in the loose edges. Then the nurse, Lauren, and I gently pull the black bag over his limp body and zip it shut.

༄ ༄

Soon, an orderly arrives to wheel Vic's body away. He is a sour-faced assistant to the Grim Reaper and doesn't look up to meet my gaze. He wheels the stretcher carrying what is left of Vic down the hall to a special elevator used for equipment and corpses, an elevator without cheerful signs of hope about support groups and upcoming lectures. As they disappear behind the elevator door, I hear again: *Gone. Gone beyond. Gone totally beyond. Oh, what an awakening!*

The hours after death are intensely sacred and startlingly ordinary. We throw away the remains of food that friends had brought but no one could eat. We pack Vic's clothes and shoes, his toothbrush and computer, and remove the photo of the Dalai Lama's embrace from the wall.

"I want to die like that," Steve says as we walk toward the parking garage.

We all do.

AFTER

6

First year. Husband dead.
Still married in dreams.

After Vic's memorial service at Wisdom's Goldenrod, I cry, walk, and talk—all three at once sometimes. Lauren and other friends come to the house and hike the trails with Daisy and me. They patiently hear my tale, even if they heard it all yesterday. They wipe my tears and invite me for dinner or take me out to lunch. David, Anthony, my brother Jim, and my cousin Tina call often. David and Anthony decide to stagger their visits so that one of them is here for three or four days each month.

My chest feels too small to hold my heart. I don't remember grief being this physical when my father died when I was fourteen. I thought heartache was merely a figure of speech.

When I'm alone, my mind cycles through the most frightening moments of Vic's illness, not his death but the cardiac arrests and the suffering of that winter. I sit on the ground in the gardens and pull weeds. I feed Daisy, the hummingbirds, and the finches. I cook vegetables from the garden, make salads, and give away the rest of what I grow. I watch the bluebirds and tree swallows as they come and go from the nesting boxes. I sit in meditation, watch sunsets, and try to absorb Vic's absence. None of this seems real.

Calming myself with deep breathing, I contemplate Rilke's words:

> Breath, you invisible poem!
> Pure, continuous exchange
> With all that is, flow and counterflow
> Where rhythmically I come to be.[11]

Because I breathe in a constant interaction with life, I am. I saw what happened when the rhythmic exchange ended.

On June 11, 2008, eight days after Vic's death, I have my first dream as a widow: I am in a wooden house. It's cluttered. The room where I will sleep is small, white-walled, and bare with a single bed. I walk up a wide wooden staircase to a landing. Through an open door, I see a giant man sitting in a porcelain claw-foot bathtub. His bronze hair looks like foliage. Water droplets cover his pale jade body. "What's with your skin?" I ask. "It lasts one year," he answers. I know that this is the Green Man. I will live in his house for a year.

When I wake up, I feel as though I have met a trustworthy guide, but I don't know just who he is. I vaguely recall a mythological god of vegetative growth and rebirth, the opposite of my death-filled mind. What could it mean that I will live in his realm for a year? I feel sure this dream god is an ally and will help me survive, although I don't know how.

"I own a book about the Green Man," Lenore Olmstead says after I tell the dream at mythology class.

Within a few days, Lenore shows up at my house with a book by William Anderson called *Green Man: The Archetype of our Oneness with the Earth*. The cover shows a sculpted face from a thirteenth-century village church in England. The leafy locks surrounding his head remind me of the man in my dream. Inside the book, there are hundreds of images of this pagan god who presided over the cycles of nature in pre-Christian Northern Europe. He survived because artisans carved and painted his image in the decorative vines and vegetation of Christian cathedrals, quietly bringing the old pagan image into the new order. His face emerges from swirls of leaves. Vines or branches grow out of his mouth or curl around his ears. Sometimes he appears with the Earth Mother or the Virgin Mary.

I talk to my therapist Barbara about the dream and read anything I can find about the Green Man. I find pictures of him on the web and paint my own images of the man who appeared in my dream.

A fresh promise of life permeates my circle of gloom. I look for wildflower buds, uncurling leaves, and the growing shoots of pine trees. It seems auspicious that my two-hundred-year-old farmhouse is the color of spruce.

On the trails, I see the Green Man's hand everywhere, pushing the June earth toward growth and life. I remember planting hundreds of seedlings with Vic and cleaning up piles of tires and the rusted bodies of abandoned cars wedged between young oak trees in the woods. I remember Vic and our sons opening new trails along the streams and clearing brushy areas in the rolling fields to save the sunset views. Vic loved and reclaimed this land. He cleared trails to the largest oaks and hickories so we could touch the bark and look up at the sky through the spreading branches. Like the Green Man, his mark is everywhere.

Nature will save me. The Green Man came to tell me so. Vic and I walked this land and breathed in beauty and solace. We prayed for strength on the red oak knoll. This year like every other, the bluebirds and the yellow trout lilies show me that fresh possibility follows bitter winter. Vic is gone and I'm not far behind, but this land cycles on, and for now I live here, anchored and supported by this verdant earth.

<h4 align="center">❧ ❧</h4>

Cleaning out Vic's desk, I find a package of promotional photos I took of him in 2001. Bored with posing, he had ducked under the branches of a red maple, poked his face through the maroon and emerald leaves, and grinned at me. I snapped the photo and forgot it until now. But there he is: my husband in his guise as the Green Man.

When I was a young woman, Vic persuaded me to wade barefoot in icy mountain streams, canoe in the buggy Canadian wilderness, and hike at the Continental Divide. He inspired my longing to own property, and his desire led us to these forests, open rolling fields, and thirty-mile views. To the world, Vic was a teacher, writer, academic, and spiritual practitioner. To me, he was a nature mystic, ecologist, and woodsman.

My husband is gone, but the Green Man remains to guide me back to Life.

≪§ §≫

Two weeks after Vic's death, the lupines burst in purple ecstasy. Near the house, bluebirds and swallows feed their broods from dawn until dusk. Male hummingbirds spend hours tracing U-shaped swoops near the sugar-water feeders, chirping warnings at each other. The forest birds give free morning and evening concerts.

The beauty that surrounds me makes a small dent in my numb confusion, but it doesn't touch the fear that tightens my shoulders. I'm afraid to live on this land alone, not because of thieves or invaders or isolation, but because I'm accustomed to mounds of firewood appearing magically in the barn, cut by Vic. I'm used to living with a guy who could fix most anything or find the right person to do the job. He arranged to have the septic pumped and climbed on a ladder to inspect the roof. I did my share to make this place hum, but how can I possibly handle Vic's chores, too? My free-floating anxiety settles on the trails where the wild grass grows by inches every night.

Although Vic mowed the hiking paths in late May and David mowed them a week ago, the weeds reach above my boot tops. *Where are you,*

Vic, keeper of well-groomed trails? The plants will soon be a foot high and, shortly after that, they will devour the footpaths that lead through the fields to the woods.

What was my excuse for refusing to take on the tractor? The Kubota was Vic's baby, and its mysterious gears, levers, and gaseous roars frightened me. They still do. Why didn't I find out how to use the diesel-fueled generator or the front loader? Why didn't I ask when the house will need a new roof or when the septic tank needs pumping? With my anxiety escalating, I swallow down the flood of fear, pull on my overalls and work boots, grab a wide-brimmed hat, and head for the barn.

Vic's absence smacks me the moment I open the barn door. I glimpse fleeting memories of him changing the tractor oil and tidying the shelves of engine lubricants and tools. The mound of drying firewood and the diesel fuel smell like Vic's work clothes. His orange Kubota is parked next to the woodpile where he always left it. The top of the rear tractor tire comes just below my shoulder, and the beast is as long as a car with an extra eight feet of brush mower attached to the back.

It's too big and I'm too little, but I'll feel better if I know how to take care of this place. Even with help from David, Anthony, and hired men. I can't stay here if I feel helpless and worried. Try! Not tomorrow. Now!

I find the key in its hiding place and hoist myself aboard the tractor seat, warily eyeing the levers, knobs, and pedals. I read the labels, study the arrows and diagrams, release the brake, and turn the key. The engine belches to life, shooting an alarming cloud of black smoke from the exhaust pipe. I hold my breath until the diesel smoke clears. Then I strap on the seat belt, shift into forward, and drive out the barn door in the lowest gear, creeping toward the head of the trail, jerking along with too much clutch and too much accelerator. Remembering Vic's instructions, I wait a few minutes to warm the engine. Then I lower the bush hog to the earth, turn on its clattering rotary blade, and drive down the trail, white knuckles latched to the steering wheel, a path of cut grass in my wake.

I soften my grip and relax my belly as I ride down the hill below the barn. *This isn't hard. What was I worried about?*

The tractor suddenly shudders to a halt with a sickening noise of metal grinding against something unyielding and solid. The bush hog groans. The tractor sputters and stalls. I wait a few seconds, trying to compose myself before turning the key to restart the engine. I turn the key. Silence.

Fearing catastrophe, I had tucked my cell phone in the front pocket of my Bib overalls before leaving the house. Sitting on the dead tractor with a sinking sense of doom in my chest, I do something I never do. I call David at work.

"I've ruined the tractor. It won't start." I can't hide the tears in my voice.

"It's OK, Mom." David laughs. "You probably had the blade too low and hit a stump. Is the bush hog blade turned on?"

"Yes, of course." *I'm not that dumb.*

"OK. Turn it off. Is the deck lifted?"

"No."

"Lift the deck off the ground with the handle next to the seat. Now turn the key, and the tractor should start. Drive ahead of the stump and drop the deck back to the ground, a little higher than before. Turn on the mower, and go. Next time, you'll remember where that stump is."

The tractor starts. I'm an eight-year-old climbing back on her bike after a terrifying spill. I'm sixteen, passing my driver's test after failing the first time. I'm a cowgirl riding bareback on a bucking bull. I can handle bumps and stumps, tall brush and blocked trails, and I will learn to haul firewood, too. I am a warrior.

I finish the main paths, driving the tractor up and down the hills and around the curves like an expert. Ten days later, I cut the trails again and continue to mow overgrown areas that Vic let go the last two years. I know exactly what to do.

⚘ ⚘

Since Vic's death forty-nine days ago, I've been reading his dog-eared and extensively annotated copy of *The Tibetan Book of Living and Dying*, a text he used in his Tibet class. The book discusses death from the perspectives of Buddhism and hospice. I pore over advice to the bereaved.

> . . . whatever you do, don't shut off your pain; accept your
> pain and remain vulnerable. However desperate you become,
> accept your pain as it is, because it is in fact trying to hand
> you a priceless gift: the chance of discovering, through spiritual
> practice, what lies behind sorrow. Rumi wrote: "Grief can be the
> garden of compassion." If you keep your heart open through
> everything, your pain can become your greatest ally in your
> life's search for love and wisdom.12

It doesn't seem possible to shut off my pain, although I would step back from it if I could. My body recoils from the persistent raw grief and tears and my muscles ache from sleeplessness. My mind is foggy and my heart feels heavy and swollen. I'm disoriented, perched on a ledge that sometimes feels closer to death than life. Even though I watch my life from a distance and nothing that happens seems to matter, something in me resists falling over that ledge. Humans endure much harder experiences than this. I want to live. I got through yesterday remembering I had made it through the day before. I will get through today.

Sometimes when I'm in the woods or watching the sun set, a wave of relief washes over me. Vic's loving eyes are gone, but those eyes had become pools of anguish. He is no longer suffering, and I am no longer witnessing his battle. Death won on the physical level, as it always does. His life had a sense of completion with no mess left behind. My pain is the ordinary suffering of those who grieve. I will survive.

According to Tibetan Buddhism, the deceased completes the after-death experience forty-nine days after death and is reborn in a new mother's womb. For Tibetans, this transition between the two lives is a time of prayers and special rituals to help the reincarnated one begin a new birth and to help the living release the dead.

I find Tibetan rituals compelling the way dreams are compelling. I don't think in terms of truth or objectivity. I'm not even sure I believe in reincarnation. I want a ceremony that has meaning for me rather than following the prescribed details of a religious plan.

In this spirit, I invite twenty women to my land for a community ritual of release on July 21. I ask that they bring something to symbolize what they need to leave behind. Most of these women have been friends for thirty or even forty years. Many of them have been part of the mythology class and the rest are members of Wisdom's Goldenrod. We meditated and studied together, raised our children and suffered losses together. They stood close to me through Vic's dying and are still nearby.

My friends and I gather in a circle beside my voluptuous vegetable garden. As we walk through the fields, Jayne Demakos, the musical director at Hospicare in Ithaca, sings a twelfth-century sacred prayer in her reedy alto voice, accompanying herself on a harmonium. After her song, we walk toward the woods in silence. We encircle the red oak knoll where Vic and I held a ritual with friends for the land after signing a conservation easement in 2005. It is where Geshe Kunkhen chanted to strengthen the healing Dakinis, where David, Anthony, and I plan to bury Vic's ashes. Then we walk five more minutes and gather at a stone fire pit bordered by flagstone benches and shaded by an ancient pine, a site that Anthony built with his friends at least ten years ago.

We offer prayers to the four directions and build an altar—a bowl of earth from my garden, a feather for air, water from the stream, and the bonfire that I light. We encircle the fire in silence, holding hands.

Janet Wylde reads a poem by an American Indian woman that she read at Vic's memorial service. The words pierced through my haze on that day.

> . . . I kept walking on this road towards You.
> . . . Until I began to hear the Song of the Mother,
> And as the door opened, I heard her Song.
> And Her Song lifted me up, so I could soar.[13]

Each woman says a few words about what she wants to release and makes her offering to the fire. I burn a copy of a photo of Vic when he was swollen and red with illness.

"May I surrender to what has died in me and allow a new life to begin."

I pull a tiny jar from my pocket, unscrew the lid, and pour a few tablespoons of clear salty liquid into the fire. The flames sizzle. Following Lauren's suggestion, I had collected my tears the last few days by holding this jar under my eyes as I cried.

"I offer my longing and grief to the fire."

We chant together and let the syllables echo through the forest. *Om Mani Padme Hum.* Lauren reads the Heart Sutra, her voice strong and sure as though she is sending the words to other worlds. She repeats the lines that circled through my mind during Vic's dying: *Gone, Gone, Gone Beyond. Gone totally beyond. Oh, what an awakening!*

After we walk back to the house, my friends lay a feast of colorful salads, bread, cheese, hummus, and homemade desserts. I feel held in love and reassured as we sit on the deck and watch a coral sunset.

After everyone leaves, I watch the constellations emerge in the night sky. A peaceful resignation passes through my body, relaxing my shoulders and opening my chest. Even though I know my calm won't last, tonight my human plight feels like a small and normal part of the magnificent comings and goings of this universe.

Remembering my pledge on the night of Vic's memorial service, I climb the stairs to my bedroom and dismantle the altar I had made for Vic. I don't want to let him go, even in this small symbolic way, but I need to finish the process of honoring and releasing that I began seven weeks ago.

I remove everything on the altar and lay a new white cloth. Then I build a new altar of feminine love and support—photos of my teacher Marion Woodman hugging me, my mother holding me as a child, and my grandmother. For seven weeks, I've been wearing a silver bracelet Lauren made a few days after Vic's death. She stamped it with the words,

"Death. Honor its power to take and give." I take off the bracelet and put it in front of a photo of Vic. Then I remove my wedding ring and place it inside the circle of the bracelet and pray that something useful will be born from this loss.

Feeling naked and vulnerable, I put my wedding ring back on my finger. Tonight I cannot imagine how I will endure the massive silence of my new life.

The following morning, I close Vic's cell phone account, fretting that he won't know how to call me. I know his body is gone. I witnessed his death and have lived with his absence for nearly two months, yet a little girl in me hopes for contact, not as an elusive spirit or dream character, but as a material man. For now I still walk beside him, him dead and me alive.

Three weeks later, I kneel on the forest floor before a shallow hole surrounded by oak, basswood, and hickory trees. I open the small cardboard box I carry, remove the plastic bag inside, and look at the contents for the first time. Vic's ashes are small sand-like crystals. They are the yellowed white of aging teeth and smell faintly musty. I am tempted to lick a finger and stick it into the ashes to taste them, but fear this will be going too far for David and Anthony. It might be going too far for me, too. Instead, I pour ashes into earth.

"Is that all there is?" Anthony jokes through his tears. "It's a rip-off!" David and I laugh despite ourselves.

That's all that is left of Vic's body—a quart and a half of chalky sand. That's all that will be left of my body. David's and Anthony's, too.

I had imagined scattering Vic's ashes on top of the earth, but my sons had a better idea. They want their father's ashes nestled in the roots of the trees and marked with a cairn. Anthony began selecting boulders from the creek bed two months ago, the day after Vic died. This steamy August morning, the two brothers used the tractor to drag the rocks out of the gully along the stream to this high spot in the forest.

Over the ashes, they construct a triangular base with three thick slabs of native flagstone. On top of the flat base, they place three granite boulders, pushed here from Canada by glaciers in the last ice age. On top of the boulders, I help them balance four smaller granite stones with the smallest perched on top. We dismantle the rocks and reposition them a few times before we have a stable structure about three feet tall standing at the top of this forest knoll where a red oak stands sentry. This massive oak was Vic's tree, the one he hugged for strength when he felt broken, the one he and I leaned into from either side, pressing our hearts and cheeks against the rough bark, reaching out to encircle the tree with our arms and grasp each other's warm hands. On one of our last walks, Vic reminded me to place his ashes here.

After the cairn is stable and balanced, David lays a red gladiola from my garden on an exposed shelf of flagstone. This will be a good place to bring my sorrow. Anthony places the unused granite boulders around the cairn to make seats where we can rest.

In a quivering voice, I read:

> It's possible I am pushing through solid rock
> in flintlike layers, as the ore lies, alone;
> I am such a long way in I see no way through,
> and no space: everything is close to my face,
> and everything close to my face is stone.
>
> I don't have much knowledge yet in grief
> so this massive darkness makes me small.
> You be the master: make yourself fierce, break in:
> then your great transforming will happen to me,
> and my great grief cry will happen to you.[14]

Anthony reads a section from *The Tibetan Book of Living and Dying* and David reads "Kindness," the poem that taught us so much the last two years.

With tears rolling down our cheeks, we hold hands around Vic's sim-ple marker and sing "Let It Be." In a recent dream, I heard this song many times by a choir of harmonizing voices. My therapist Barbara reminded me to look up the lyrics.

David's rich baritone voice takes the lead and he knows all the words.

I startle awake at three a.m., driving through a tornado looking for Vic. In some dreams, I search through hospital rooms or hotels alarmed that Vic needs me and I can't find him. *Why did I let him out of my sight? Where is he? Is he alive or dead?*

Two or three nights a week, dream Vic visits and reassures me. He holds me or lies with his head on my lap. Sorrow tinges these scenes, since something in me knows what has happened in my waking world.

In these night visitations, I grapple with the paradox of Vic's physical death standing alongside his continuing presence in my thoughts. Vic is both here and gone, healthy and sick, alive and dead. Part of me wants to stay with him; part of me knows this is not possible. In one dream, I convince his doctors that, even though Vic is walking around, he is actually dead. "There was a memorial service. I have a death certificate to prove it," I tell them. In another, I cry out to Vic, "Don't you know how much I love you? But you can't stay. I can't be married to a dead person."

I dream that I stand at the kitchen sink in pajamas. Vic murmurs lovingly into my ear. I put my arms around him. His body is small, about the size of mine. We hold each other and sway back and forth. I whisper, "We have to remember how precious this is. I know what it's like to be without it."

I paint and draw my dreams, discuss them in therapy, tell them to friends, and write about them. When Vic is absent for too many nights, I worry he will disappear just as he vanished from my waking world.

Months after Vic's death, when dream Vic hasn't appeared for more than a week, I assume my grief process is moving to a new stage. That night, I dream that I'm carrying Vic's green suitcase, but he is dead and doesn't need a suitcase. I'm going on this trip alone.

∞ ∞

Steve reminds me of a two-minute YouTube clip of the Dalai Lama speaking at Colgate six weeks before Vic's death followed by an interview of Vic. After avoiding this video for months, I watch it five times.

Vic appears composed, although he held back tears with a quivering chin and tight jaw. He was swollen and obviously ill.

"In the last few years, I've gone from being the healthiest man I know to being the sickest," he explained to the interviewer. ". . . But the thing that gave me the most strength and encouragement is what the Dalai Lama spoke of today—genuine concern for other people. Not to say I can do it all that well, but I see the virtue of it. I see the lifesaving value of it."

Human kindness. It all comes down to that.

I stood at Vic's side that day, not part of the video, but next to him, watching over him, proud, exhausted, but grateful we had made it to that day so Vic could see His Holiness.

It's easy to idealize the dead. When I criticize anything about Vic, I feel I betray him, since he is no longer here to defend himself. In the last months, he didn't defend himself anyway. He had lost his mental clarity and ability to meditate, so he focused on kindness. Part of this lofty path was to accept blame. How crazy that made me when I wanted to argue and blow off steam.

Truth is, Vic was magnificent in his dying, but I tend to forget that I was equally magnificent. I put aside my twenty-year complaint that he took up too much space, laughing with him that he had finally succeeded in his unconscious desire to be the complete focus of our life together. Like a sick child, he needed constant attention. Usually I could provide that, although sometimes I had nothing left to give.

One October night in 2007, we got an eight o'clock call from Michael Eisman suggesting that Vic take a diuretic to see if it would reverse his alarming swelling. Because Vic was too ill to drive, it was up to me to make the hour-long round trip to Ithaca and pick up the medicine—immediately since the pharmacy closed at nine.

"I don't want to drive to Ithaca. Can't you see I'm exhausted?"

"I'll ride with you," Vic offered.

"I don't want to be with you and your symptoms," I shot back at him, shocked by the words that had escaped from my mouth. "I'm not a good person. I'm not even a nice person," I cried as I ran out the door to the car.

"You have been an angel to me," Vic called after me. I turned and faced him.

"I'm not an angel. I'm just a weak bitch who's breaking under the load. I'll get your medicine. You stay here, because I can't be nice right now. I don't want to say more mean things."

I collected myself during the trip, and when I returned home, Vic waited at the door, ready to hold me in forgiving arms. Recalling that day, I forgive myself.

<6 <6

In September, I spend a few days visiting museums in New York City with Barbara Nowogrodzki. The tomb statues in the Greek collection at the Metropolitan Museum of Art fascinate me.

"I'm worried you'll fall through a crack in the sidewalk," Barbara tells me as we walk along the avenues. I've leaned on her since Vic got sick. I worry about being a burden, but she and others keep a close eye on me. I will not disappear.

In October, I drive to Sayre, Pennsylvania, with Lenore to canvas for Obama. Most people don't answer or they shut the door in my face, but a few want more information. No one asks how I'm doing. No one notices that I'm dazed and only half present. I am anonymous and invisible, except to Lenore who squeezes my hand, her soft brown eyes squinting with empathy. Walking from one house to the next, I watch Lenore's brown curls bounce along as she moves down the opposite side of the street. I watch her gesture and smile at whomever answers the door, while I knock and hope no one is home so I can leave a flyer under the doormat and move on. If a door opens, I make it through the script given out by the organizers. It is good to do something that matters, but mostly I need to walk and be with Lenore.

∽ ∾

When cold weather hits in November, I begin to dread Christmas. I've always bought gifts, decorated the house, and cooked, but I'd rather hide in the cellar this year. Johanna Goehner generously invites my family to join hers for Christmas Eve. David and Anthony will be home at the same time for the first time since we buried Vic's ashes. I buy groceries, hang a few lights from the windows, and hope for the best.

The night David arrives, we get heavy snow. His two dogs have been in the car for the long drive from North Carolina, so he lets them loose for a romp. The younger dog Mandy returns, but Shelly doesn't. I call her name into the bitter wind, while David drives up and down the road in his truck.

Not this. We can't take another loss.

I sleep fitfully, and in the morning David starts looking as soon as the snowplows go by. It's ten degrees and windy. Snowbanks are piled high on my country road. David drives up and down in his pickup truck, honking and watching. Suddenly, about a quarter mile from home, his little black dog shoots out from behind a snowdrift. David opens the truck door and she jumps in as though nothing has happened.

"Where were you last night, Shelly?" we ask as she wags her tail and devours breakfast.

Thank you, Great Mother, for helping Shelly make it through the night.

Vic's absence fills the house, so I'm glad to go out on Christmas Eve.

At Johanna's home, we sit at a festive table with candles and Christmas lights. I hand out gifts of wool socks and chocolate and Johanna's husband Werner pours the red wine. We eat and drink too much, but David, Anthony, and I are gloomy company anyway. I'm grateful to Johanna and her daughters Anna and Sophia who care for us and entertain Virginia, Vic's mom, but I want to go home and cry. The Goehners do all they can, but I feel we have spoiled their holiday.

Christmas morning, David, Anthony, and I drive half an hour to Ithaca and make breakfast at Virginia's apartment. We've used up our pretend celebration energy and want to crawl into separate corners, so we return home by noon. Virginia prefers to be alone with her grief and is ready for us to go. I take a long walk in the woods with Daisy and make pasta with tomato sauce I froze in August. We're glad to end this day.

"We made it through," I say. "It stunk, but we made it."

"It will be easier next year," David tells me.

Maybe.

❦ ❧

In March, I join a new writing class. Writing has always helped me work through problems and I've attended a writing group since September with an excellent teacher. But my emotional pieces about my marriage and Vic's death feel out of place. I experiment with other topics, but I'm only interested in exploring grief.

My therapist Barbara suggests Ellen Schmidt's "Writing through the Rough Spots" since classes are small and Ellen invites exploration of hard topics. With Ellen, I write about Vic's illness and death and weep as I read out loud. Ellen hears the stories beneath my emotions and encourages me to keep going. In the intimate classes around her table, my grieving voice finds words and stories. I feel welcome and safe.

I want to do something worthwhile, so I spend a morning at the local Head Start program thinking I'll volunteer there. The children's noise and chaos grates against my introverted grief, and I can hardly wait to escape their shrill exuberance. Within a few days, I talk to the volunteer coordinator at Hospicare in Ithaca, imagining myself pulling weeds in the hospice gardens.

"Obviously, I can't work with sick people or families," I tell the volunteer coordinator Wendy Yettru at the end of our weepy interview.

"It's OK if you cry here. We all cry," she assures me. "How are you with computers?"

"I use my computer every day."

"Would you like to volunteer for me?" she asks. "I need help with data entry. I think we can work together."

"I'd love to be the volunteer coordinator's volunteer," I say, grateful she has a job for me. We make an appointment to begin my training in a week.

"Haven't you had enough death?" Anthony asks when I tell him I'm volunteering at Hospicare.

"It feels just right," I tell him. "I need to be with people who know death is an every day thing, and I need to do something for someone else."

With a writing class and a volunteer gig in place, I decide Daisy and I need a new dog friend. On a cold February day, we meet a two-year-old male Labrador retriever who lives in a foster home. Jackson is a gorgeous yellow Lab, a large version of Daisy; but Daisy averts her gaze from his rowdy energy. As Jackson pulls me down the road on a leash, I decide Daisy is right. We simply don't have enough energy for this guy.

While the Green Man slumbers under the snow, I track paw and hoof prints as Daisy roots around for deer scat and sniffs at the mosses that dare to turn green on the south sides of oak trees. I order vegetable seeds and make root cuttings to plant when the weather warms. The days lengthen and my calendar fills with activities, but I feel only half present. My world is a flat black and white screen that cannot draw my attention away from the alluring colors of the past.

⤸ ⤷

"If you only love yourself half as much as I love you, you'll be OK," Vic said hundreds of times. Self-love demands acceptance rather than judgment. It asks me to soften to myself. It asks me to accept this great grief without apologizing for the support I need from my sons or weepy late-night phone calls to friends. It asks me to be kind to the little child in me who cries out lost and abandoned. Is it possible to love myself just half as much as Vic loved me? Maybe. Possibly. I hope so.

A Korean Zen teacher told Anthony that he will experience his father's love everywhere now. That seems possible, too. If I can stay with this grief and allow my heart to crack open, if I can keep myself from shutting down and denying what I feel, then I might learn something about a wider love. Sometimes, mourning feels like a spiritual pilgrimage. On these days, I know grief is a sacred thing, teaching more about love than I would have learned in a life without cancer, suffering, and death. Life is prayer. Love is a blessing. Mortality is my teacher. If I stay with this grief, I might learn what it means to be an open-hearted, compassionate human being.

As the spring days lengthen, I yearn to fall in love with life. After my dad died when I was fourteen, my mutt Amigo comforted me by pressing his body into mine as I sat on the floor doing homework. Fourteen years later in 1973, Vic and I bought a black Labrador retriever, the first in a long line of Labs that soothed our family, played with us, and insisted on frequent walks. I visit a promising litter of puppies with Lauren, but decide I can't support a dog breeding factory. I look online and answer ads, but nothing feels right.

In April, I drive to North Carolina with Daisy to visit David and his two terrific rescue dogs. David and I visit local dog shelters and find a young female mix. Lucy seems relaxed when David inspects her mouth and touches her toes. She leans reassuringly into my thigh.

"She's the nicest dog in the place," the dog warden assures me. Still, I hesitate. He knows nothing about this dog's history.

On Monday, I revisit the dog and take Daisy to meet her. The shelter dog's eyes are desperate after being caged for three days. She jumps on Daisy playfully, but calms down when I distract her with a dog cookie. The three of us spend an hour in a small visitors' room at the shelter. The dog knows no commands and won't chase a ball, but she relaxes as I pet her and leans into my leg again. Daisy seems fine with her, so I decide I can make this work.

That night I dream that a group of dogs wants to be happy—surely a positive sign.

Tuesday morning I collect our new dog Lucy and drive eleven hours home. Daisy wedges herself against Lucy's crate, snuggling as close to Lucy as she can get. That night, under the calming influence of doggie snores, I sleep better than I have in months.

Lucy is a headstrong, untrained girl, just as I expected. The first day, I take her for frequent leashed walks in the field and begin teaching her to sit. On the second day, a lost stranger with a large dog walks across the field toward my house. The woman waves and approaches me. Without warning, Lucy lunges at the woman and attacks her dog with bared teeth and snarls, almost yanking the leash from my hand.

The third day, Lucy turns on Daisy and bloodies her face and ears. I grab Lucy's collar and pull her off. Fortunately, she doesn't sink her teeth into my face.

My vet Vivien Surman, a practical, no-nonsense British woman, guesses that Lucy is as much Chow as Lab, but thinks the dog is trainable. My job is to get her used to Daisy and her new world—cautiously. Within a few weeks, I realize it isn't just dogs that Lucy wants to kill. She is after snakes, birds, cows, horses, and cats, anything that moves. I'm scared for Daisy and keep the dogs in separate rooms unless Lucy is crated.

A dog trainer, who is also Vivien's veterinary assistant, is sure Lucy can be taught to accept other dogs; but first I hire a dog behaviorist and work with Lucy at home. I'm advised to walk as a family, so I put Daisy on a leash on my right side while Lucy walks on the left—incessantly tugging. Outdoors, Lucy is too distracted by her attempts to escape to attack Daisy who becomes nervous and fearful. I rent whole seasons of Cesar Millan's *Dog Whisperer* and study his techniques, soon realizing I am no Cesar Millan. No matter how much we train, Lucy accelerates from calm to crazed in seconds with no obvious provocation.

At the first dog class, I keep Lucy far from the other dogs, walking her back and forth and reassuring her; but she rears on her hind legs, lunges, and snarls. I teach Lucy to wear a muzzle. She doesn't mind her muzzle, as though she's worn one before. She calms down—slightly—so the trainer hopes that fear is driving her aggression. After more weeks of classes, the trainer allows muzzled Lucy off leash with a docile dog that Lucy has been around since the first class. Lucy attacks while the frightened dog averts his eyes and cowers in submission. Even though my dog is muzzled, my heart pounds with fear. How can I live with this devil?

Three months after adopting Lucy, during my fourth veterinary consultation about her behavior, the trainer and Dr. Surman tell me Lucy is ruining Daisy's life and mine and will harm an animal or even a human. They suggest euthanasia.

No! I can't. I believe in nonviolence. I'm a vegetarian, and I love dogs. I can't kill a healthy dog, not even a crazed one. Or can I?

"Now that I know her better, I wonder if this dog was trained to fight," Dr. Surman says. "My guess is she didn't work out, so they dumped her."

I sit across the stainless examination table with these two kind women and weep helplessly, but I am not blameless. After forty years of gentle Labs, it was naïve to adopt a shelter dog with an unknown history when I know nothing about mistreated, untrained, or aggressive dogs. I only know about gentle eight-week-old Labs bought from backyard breeders. Vic would never have made such a sentimental choice, but I did.

"Leave her here," the vet suggests.

"I need a few days," I decide. I take Lucy home and watch for a positive sign from the Divine Deity of Dogs, but no sign comes. Lucy pulls, snarls, and snaps at Daisy. Like Psyche feeding Cerberus, the three-headed guard dog of the Greek underworld, I soothe Lucy with marrow bones and extra food. Inwardly I give up.

"You need to leave," Dr. Surman says when I drop Lucy off a few days later. "Your grief makes it harder for Lucy. She isn't afraid of me, so let me handle this."

I did not do the crazy things that women do after their husband's die. I did not sell the property for a song or run off with a snake charmer, but I did adopt Lucy. I am humiliated by my stupidity and horrified by the outcome. This wild beast is a product of my grief and desperation, an expression of my own feral emotions. Instead of falling in love, I feel like a criminal.

⤳ ⤲

After building a nest in the birdhouse in April, the female bluebird fails to settle in. Her hopeful mate dances on the roof and encourages her with worms.

"Well-located home still available," he chirps, but she disappears. He comes around a few more times but finally moves on, too. Did wild Lucy's training walks in the yard disturb the bluebirds? Did the tractor get too close, or was a hawk eyeing them from overhead? I want the bluebirds to come back, but for now, they are gone.

It's been hard to get started on the flower and vegetable beds this spring. It is the Green Man's season, but who will eat this food? Who will look at all these flowers?

"Start something, even if you don't care about it now," David advises. "Remember what you used to enjoy and do it. Then when you're ready, something you always loved will be waiting for you."

Gardening has calmed and nurtured me since my dad helped me plant my first radishes and carrots in the backyard in seventh grade. I know my friend Steve, master gardener that he is, would help if I asked, but I don't call him.

As the weather warms, I lethargically eye the grass that consumes my favorite flower bed, the perennial garden of daffodils, poppies, lilies, and iris that sits on a hillside outside the big window in the kitchen. I let all the flower beds go the last few years, but this one is the worst. The perennials try to force their way through the grass mat, but I don't have the will to help them.

Tuesday morning, Anthony's shoes are by the front door. He flew in last night from San Francisco. I didn't hear him come in after midnight, since Daisy didn't bark.

"What needs doing?" he asks after he drinks a few cups of coffee and cooks himself some eggs.

We rake out the vegetable garden and plant lettuce, peas, and onions. After lunch, we tackle the perennial flower bed and dig out three-quarters of the weeds before giving up. Wednesday, after we finish the main flower bed, Anthony turns to pruning and trail maintenance in the woods while I plant chard and escarole. In the evening, we sit on the front steps and admire our work.

"It's hard to know why I bother," I whimper.

Anthony puts his arm around me and pulls me into his side, reminding me that I bother because this is our family place, transformed again by young male energy, persistent habits, and love.

May 7, 2009

Dearest Vic,

This morning, I saw a turkey strut, a huge tom with his fan of iridescent feathers, desperately trying to impress the hens. Unconvinced, they turned tail on him and pecked through the grass. Robins dance on the paths, their red breasts flashing in the morning light. I want to call out to you and share what I see. I want to hand you the binoculars or watch you focus the telescope as you did last spring.

The wild lupines spread through the fields. Your favorite lilacs and iris bud, even though you aren't here to admire them. Everything on this land reminds me of you.

I'm exhausted with grieving. The more fatigued I become, the more I submit to the downward pull. I am in the Underworld with Orpheus and Eurydice. Like Eurydice, you must stay in the Land of Shades. Like Orpheus, I keep looking back. Still, I am forced to leave you behind and return to life and sing my lament to love.

I have no regrets, dear Vic. We did all we could to help you live and thrive. We loved each other so fiercely that you worried about how I would be without you. I promised I would be OK, and I am keeping my promise, but I want more than survival. I want to be a wiser woman because of this initiation.

I bow my head in submission, slowly accepting there is no escape from the pain, no escape for anyone. I cling to a favorite quote from Rilke, the one that helps me endure as it helped you endure.

> . . . How dear you will be to me then, you nights
> of anguish. Why didn't I kneel more deeply to accept you,
> inconsolable sisters, and, surrendering, lose myself
> in your loosened hair. How we squander our hours of pain.
> How we gaze beyond them into the bitter duration
> to see if they have an end. Though they are really
> our winter-enduring foliage, our dark evergreen,
> one season in our inner year-, not only a season
> in time-, but are place and settlement, foundation and soil
> and home.[15]

I am still a novice in the lessons of grief. I pray my heart will open wide enough to hold your death and then open wider still to help hold the world's suffering. I pray for the capacity to welcome life's surprising and joyful gifts, rather than waste my days yearning for the past. You would want this for me. I want it for myself.

Thank you, dear Vic, for loving all the good and bad in me as you did, and thank you for giving me the opportunity to love all of you. We have been so lucky!

Your loving E

PS. Last night we made wet, wild love on the kitchen floor, and then I woke up. Thanks for stopping by.

7

Second year. Drowning in sorrow.
Rescued by friends.

Nearly a year after Vic's death, the wild lupines erupt with thousands of promising flower stalks. Vic and I planted pounds of wildflower seeds in our fields over the years. The grasses devoured most of them, but lupines thrived and spread from original patches to cover broad areas on the hillsides with tall purple spikes. This spring, they push their way through my numb despair. Life goes on, they insist. Open your eyes. There is joy here.

I invite my community for a walk to mark the first anniversary of Vic's death on June 3. David and Anthony will come home to be part of the day, and Vic's mom Virginia will join us. My friends from the mythology class offer to organize a dish-to-pass vegetarian feast with plenty of local Finger Lakes wine. I need a day of remembrance, but even more a day of thanks for my friends, my sons, the Green Man, and the land that held and soothed me this year.

Throughout an afternoon of sunshine and soft breezes, people arrive to celebrate Vic's life and admire the flowers. Some walk alone in walking meditation, some laugh in small groups, and some move silently, holding hands. They stroll along trails bordered by lupines and daisies, heading for the oak knoll where we buried Vic's ashes.

As some friends begin their walk, they pass others returning to the house for wine and food. I walk toward the woods with one group for a while and then turn to walk back toward the house with another. I spend the afternoon strolling back and forth through the fields, greedily devouring hugs and love, admiring my smiling friends in their pastel summer clothes, and adoring the purple lupines. Eventually I make it to the oak knoll where people sit quietly on granite stones, tree trunks, and the forest floor. Serenaded by birds, we circle the cairn where Vic's ashes are buried, absorbing his absence and the mystery of what remains.

David and Anthony dreaded this day, imagining a somber affair with a weeping mother and an avalanche of sympathetic, solicitous looks from people they hadn't seen since Vic's memorial service. Instead, we celebrate that we are here together and that Vic was once here, too.

"It's wonderful to see you smile," David says as he pulls me close in a warm hug.

A few days later, I grab a rake and bags of lupine and northeast wildflower seeds and walk with Daisy to a freshly burned brush pile near the entry to the woods. Vic and I piled fallen branches here a few years ago, and Anthony burned the dry brush before he left yesterday. I rake the charred bed, fling seeds in every direction, and press them into the soil with my boots, remembering that the Earth does the real work. As the farmer, I only encourage the process.

> Even as the farmer labors
> There where the seed turns into summer,
> It is not his work. It is Earth who gives.[16]

❧ ☙

I'm an exercise trainer and a nutritionist, so I know how to take care of the body, but I forget why my health matters. Who cares about extra pounds and tight pants? Why not eat a late night bagel or a bowl of granola in exchange for a moment's pleasure or an hour of numbing satiety?

I tell myself what I once told my nutrition and exercise clients. *The smallest challenges feel insurmountable when you abandon your body. Movement makes your body sing and calms your mind. What good can you do in this life if you're unhealthy?*

I returned to my exercise room a few weeks after Vic's death, inspired by his unending efforts to maintain his strength. After that first gentle strength-training session, I felt a flicker of hope.

While Vic was sick and since his death, I walked twice a day—sometimes fast aerobic walks, but usually slow explorations that connected me to the cycles of the land. Watching one season move into another, I knew death was as ordinary as life, a natural ending as well as the beginning of something new.

Eating well came harder than exercise. Grandma's cherry pies and buttermilk biscuits had eased me through my dad's death when I was a teenager, but I didn't care about food for a few weeks after Vic's death. Although many mourners have trouble swallowing the smallest bites, my empty ache soon clamored to be filled. My good habits didn't abandon me completely. I ate oats for breakfast, vegetables from the garden for lunch, and salad for dinner as I had done for many years; but late-night extras made me feel like I'd given up on myself.

Now, I have conversations with the child in me who wants to be pacified with sweets and grains. She's the inconsolable one who can't stop crying. She complains that she's had enough pain and doesn't deserve more punishment. In my imagination, I pick her up in my arms and tell her I will take care of her. She doesn't trust me. When I banish sweets, she wants to gobble chocolate.

"You only want to shut me up and make me shape up," she whines.

"I'm trying to love you," I tell her. I know she teaches me to care for my deep sadness and helplessness.

I imagine carrying her on my right hip the way my mother carried me. The little one pouts and watches me with suspicion. Slowly she dares to hope that I will befriend her. I promise not to force rigid food rules on her, but I've made and broken that promise many times. I promise to take time to paint with watercolors, work a jigsaw puzzle with Gita and Lourdes, or lie on the floor hugging Daisy. I promise if she wants a muffin, I will listen rather than screaming no or letting her stuff the muffin down without tasting it. I remind her I can love her and care for her even if I can't let the three-year-old within me make all the decisions.

She and I learned much about suffering these past few years. We need to hold on to each other. When I tend her with kindness, I feel Vic close by, standing between us and holding each of us by the hand, connecting us to each other to help me heal this broken girl, this broken me.

ᢍ ᢌ

"Are you still looking for a Lab puppy?" I'm asked by email at the end of June. "You contacted me about six months ago. I have a litter of chocolates just a few days old. They'll be ready by the end of August."

"Yes." I hit reply and send, leaping out of my desk chair with excitement.

Despite the failure with Lucy, I want a new dog; but this time I need a sure thing, so I'll raise a pup from the start. The breeder runs a small family business with only a few litters a year, and the pup won't be ready for two months, so I have time to rethink this move.

Yes, yes, yes. I want a sweet puppy, a reliable well-tempered Lab, Vic's and my favorite breed. After dealing with Lucy, raising a puppy will be easy.

Eight-week-old Willow comes home with Daisy and me the last day of August. The next day, I take the pup to my volunteer shift at Hospicare. People stop by the volunteer desk to give her a cuddle and introduce themselves. I feel the promise of love and life.

ᢍ ᢌ

I decide to have our second Christmas without Vic at home, so I decorate the house with strings of small white lights and my favorite gaudy

Mexican Christmas ornaments. David and Anthony pick up Virginia in Ithaca and bring her home for "la Notte di Natale," the Night before Christmas. I cook the Christmas Eve feast I prepared when Vic was here—an elaborate antipasto, tofu balls, and pasta with marinara sauce—but the atmosphere is grim. I'm grateful when Steve and Janet stop by with love and distraction.

On Christmas Day, we cook brunch at Virginia's apartment. By the time David, Anthony, and I clean up, Virginia is ready to watch TV in her recliner and take a snooze. After we return home, David and Anthony pull into separate corners of the house for exercise and email. Instead of a fancy Christmas dinner, they vote for appetizers and minestrone soup. After dinner, they plan to go to a dance club in Ithaca where Anthony will play techno music for the Christmas night crowd of young people who've had enough of their families.

Standing alone, chopping garlic at the wide kitchen counter, I feel a stab of grief. If Vic were here, he would be next to me chopping salad or washing the dirty pots and bowls. He and I would be allies, talking through family tensions and expectations, sticking close to each other. Remembering my innocent happiness when Vic proposed to me on Christmas Eve in 1967, I drown in self-pity. By the time David and Anthony come downstairs to help with dinner, I'm swimming in sorrow. David stands close to me, his head bowed in sadness, while Anthony steps back, away from the brink.

"I can't deal with it," Anthony protests. "We've done a great job getting through Christmas this year, but I don't want to dig into the grief tonight."

Hot shame washes over me. Tears ooze out of my eyes, defying my effort to hold them back.

"I'm sorry, Mom," Anthony apologizes, putting his arm around my shoulders. "I was harsh. Let's just eat dinner."

"I understand. I do. My sorrow sinks everyone's ship."

"Anthony's right, Mom," David says gently. "Let's just be together. We all feel sad, but Anthony and I need a break."

"Yes. Yes. Of course," I stammer. I can't expect them to keep their footing when my avalanche comes rolling down.

The next morning, we discuss last night's bump.

"I'm sorry I was insensitive," Anthony says with defeated eyes.

"I'm sorry I'm so emotional," I tell him, swallowing my tears.

"We're all OK," David assures us. "It's a hard time of year."

Unsettled, I call Barbara Nowogrodzki after they leave for town and tell her the story.

"David and Anthony stand on the side of life and the future," she says. "They are young and this is right for them. You stand closer to death. This is where you need to be. Your family is searching for a balance between the two. You're talking it through. You're doing great."

I know she's right.

⤜ ⤛

When calm, frisky, affectionate Willow was five months old, I noticed an occasional limp. A few weeks ago, I took her to a veterinary surgeon near Syracuse who predicted she would grow out of it.

Following his instructions, I take her for two forty-five-minute leash walks a day. The limp persists. In January, I take Willow to a veterinary physical therapist in Ithaca. She gives Willow exercises for her now atrophied leg. I dutifully put Willow through the paces each day and take her to the physical therapist twice a week for water exercise. When therapy doesn't help, I make an appointment with a second veterinary surgeon, pushing away the thought that this is punishment for euthanizing Lucy.

Dr. Ross's brow knits with concern as he watches Willow walk up and down the office hallway. He is a soft-spoken, gentle, white-haired man in a white lab coat. I like the way he handles Willow's body, exploring the detailed terrain of her leg as though he is reading Braille. He soothes her with soft touches when his manipulation makes her whimper and recoil.

"What do you think?" I ask.

"We need another set of X-rays to compare with the ones taken two months ago. I'll have to anesthetize her. If there is more damage than before, I suggest doing the surgery immediately. If you'd rather wait, we can do that. It's up to you."

"I don't know what to do, so I'll do what you advise," I tell him. "But I'm going on a trip in two weeks. I'll be away for ten days. I have to go." Lourdes, Gita, Lenore, and I rented a condo for a week in Florida. I want to go, and I can't let them down.

"If she needs surgery, and I expect she does," Dr. Ross says, "she can go home with you for two weeks and then stay here while you're away. Our vet techs will take good care of her."

"She has osteochondrosis in the cartilage of that knee. The cartilage didn't mineralize into bone in one area and it's much worse than it was in the previous X-rays," Dr. Ross tells me when he calls two hours later. "Under anesthesia, without her resistance, the knee is unstable. I'm worried about the ligaments. If she were my pup, I'd operate immediately."

∽ ∾

"Things were a mess in there," he says when I pick Willow up a few days later. He shows me X-ray images on a computer screen and points out the problems. "The cartilage was inflamed. The cruciate ligament was spongy, rubbery, and torn. I couldn't save it. I removed the ligament and took a tendon from below the knee to create a new support."

"How could this happen to such a young pup?" I ask.

"I don't know," he says, shrugging his shoulders apologetically, reminding me of the shrugs of oncologists and cardiologists. "I've never done so much reconstruction on a dog this young. My best guess is that osteochondrosis caused inflammation in that knee for many months. We'll never know for sure."

Willow is confined to a crate or a four-foot leash and limited to five-minute walks outside with her hips in a sling. After a month, there will be daily exercises, water and physical therapy, and more confinement. My sweet pup, my promise of happiness, can't frolic and play. She can't run free in the woods like every other dog I've had except Lucy. Willow is an invalid.

Whoever is in charge here, I'm telling you I need a break I whine to myself, because no one else is listening.

Stuck in grief and martyrdom, I am a devotee of Our Lady of Perpetual Dissatisfaction. It's 48 degrees and gray with twenty-five mile an hour winds, not what I hoped for in late February on Gasparilla Island, Florida. I phone the veterinary office in Ithaca, and they assure me that Willow is being coddled by the vet technicians. I need to get into a vacation mood.

Despite the nasty weather, I entice Lenore, Lourdes, and Gita to visit an exposed pier where I saw a single dolphin and many pelicans yesterday. The wild creatures are not there today. Lenore pulls her wool beret down over her dark curls and suggests going back to our rented condo. She and Gita want to explore a dream series they started at home. My rational adult self understands there is plenty of time to be together, but the vulnerable child in me feels left out and about to blow. Out of mercy, Lourdes agrees to come with me to the beach despite the wild wind and threatening sky.

I drive south on the narrow island road with Lourdes in the passenger seat. The old folks are in their houses this morning, buttoning their winter sweaters rather than driving their golf carts on the roadside paths. We pass the pink stucco library and the pastel town center and enter the state beach parking lot near the lighthouse. There is one other car in the lot and no one on the beach. The surf pounds against the white sand in angry gray-green pulses, bass drum crashes that penetrate the hearing loss I've struggled with for the last ten years. I pull my winter hat down over my ears and zip my windbreaker tight under my chin.

We watch two pelicans steal fish from three intrepid fishermen in a small swaying aluminum boat. The pelicans flap their awkward wings over the boat and splash their demands. Lourdes and I laugh—my first lightness of the day.

To escape the wind, we walk along the protected harbor side of the wide white beach and soon meet a fortressed "Do Not Trespass" wall. We turn back toward the Gulf and see three white ibis poking around at water's edge for fat translucent sea fleas. Their digging beaks curve elegantly toward their chests.

We notice a few more pelicans and two black skimmers floating just above the water. I poke aimlessly through a pile of shells on the white sand and study the bird identification book, searching for the name of a brown gull-like bird with ducky feet that moves among the terns. I tuck deeper into my hood to escape the gusts.

I came here to be in community with the living, but it's easier to be with the dead and dying. I want to be with my friend Barbara whose husband was diagnosed with cancer just a few days before this trip. I want to do my volunteer shift at Hospicare and take care of wounded Willow. I want to visit Vic's cairn in my forest. Instead, I am here, trapped.

Suddenly, Lourdes yelps. Startled, I look up. There they are in frisbee-tossing distance—dolphins breaching waves that thunder through the deep channel across the southern tip of the island, moving from the Gulf of Mexico toward Charlotte Harbor. I squeal, too. Lourdes jumps up and down, flapping her arms with delight. Dolphins, many dolphins—leaping, banking, rolling, alone and in small groups. Sometimes I see only their gray backs. Sometimes they fly above the water, showing their bellies, arching like rainbows.

We stand stunned, blessed by their grace, blessed by their numbers, blessed by the emptiness of the beach as though we are the first or last humans on this white sand. Hushed, we wait, scanning the water, hoping to catch another glimpse of this waking dream. The dolphins return, six close by and two in the distance. They pierce the icy shield that surrounds my heart. For a moment, I fully admit the secret I'm trying to hide from my friends and even from myself. After all the effort and expense to make this trip happen, I don't want to be here. I don't know how to join the conversation or make myself part of this sociable group, even though these women are dear friends who don't want me to conceal my sorrow. I don't want to be difficult and take the shadow role. I want to banish my aloofness, but can't find the place in me that knows how.

We watch the dolphins for an hour while the sky breaks blue. Tourists appear on the beach in parkas and wool socks as the dolphins disappear. The quieting sea turns from roiling gray to the turquoise of Florida postcards.

Instead of last night's sorrowful dream of Vic and my restless longing for the past, I will remember dolphins breaching through dark water, luminous revelations leaping from the great unconscious sea. I will remember that my tongue tasted brine in the palm of my hand and wild birds cried out without asking anything of me. I will know that wild waves pounded against my heart and briefly broke through grief and that my friendship with these women is steadfast and resilient.

Somewhere over the rainbow
Bluebirds fly.
Birds fly over the rainbow.
Why then, oh why can't I?[17]

Bluebirds arrive a little late this spring and don't stick around to perch on the roof of their favorite nesting box. No male pushes the others aside and claims the territory. I can't watch through the telescope as a bluebird opens his chest and throws back his head in song. Sunlight doesn't flicker off iridescent blue feathers. *Don't they know I need them?* In the winter, I cleaned out all four nesting boxes, and they reject them all. *How could they?*

Unwilling to give up, I buy a new bird box. The New York State Department of Environmental Conservation guy says bluebirds like new houses better than old ones. He tells me it isn't too late because the birds are still finding nesting sites.

"Sometimes they come within hours when I put up a new house," he promises with an optimistic smile.

At home, I inspect the old weathered box, looking over the serious nails Vic used to hold it in place on the railing south of the house. I head for the garage to find similar long heavy nails and a big hammer, muttering all the way. *Screw this. I don't want to hang a birdhouse. Where is Vic? This is his job.* My jaw clenches as I paw through Vic's toolbox. *Shit.* No hammer here. I find big nails, but can't imagine whacking them without a hefty hammer. I look on the shelves, dig through other toolboxes, and even check through the tractor tools in the barn. My neck tightens, aiming for a headache.

Defeated, I head for the house to get the small finishing hammer I keep indoors. My head bows forward with effort, as though I'm walking into a stiff wind. I know the small hammer is inadequate for the job, but I am too grumpy to keep looking for the manly one. *Who moved it anyway? What right did they have to move the hammer? Where is the goddamned hammer?*

I pry the old birdhouse away from the fence post. Now there's no backing out. I lay the new box on the ground and begin whacking to get the nails started, but the angle is wrong and I smack the front of the birdhouse as often as I hit the nails. The more I hammer, the less effective my whacks become. *Shit. Shit. I hate this.* I try bending the nails, but they don't budge. I put the birdhouse up against the railing anyway and take a few more whacks. *You don't have to do this. You're choosing this. You can stop and wait until Anthony comes next week. You can ask for help. Why don't you let it go?*

Screw you, I say to that know-it-all voice. My jaws clench. Slam, hit. Slam, miss. Slam, dent the birdhouse. The nail barely moves as the railing gives with each strike. I remember holding that railing in place as Vic hammered in the old birdhouse. *Where is he?* I pound, miss, hit, and curse. My head throbs with each strike.

Stupid. This is stupid. I hate this life. Where is Vic? I'm ten years old, and I want my daddy. I'm sixty-four years old, and I want my old life. Tears drip into my glasses. I wipe my nose on my sleeve. *It's hot, damn it. Too hot for April. I'm sick of being a crybaby. I'm sick of being sad about everything. Shit. I refuse to give up.*

Slowly, I hammer the nails into place. The birdhouse stands upright and straight, a minor miracle. I'm exhausted, but I forced my way through—will and push, try, try, never give up. I return the tools to the box in the garage and look around again for the large hammer. *Where is it? Screw this. I hate this.*

I sit on the front steps of the sidewalk and cry. My body slumps under the weight of bitterness and self-reproach.

Suck it up and grow up, the inner judge demands.

Screw you, you bully, yells the angry girl.

Sometimes I was angry during Vic's illness, but I've seldom been angry since his death. Why am I pissed off now about stupid things? I don't want to be a victim of anger, but the complaints insist on rolling out. I don't want to smash nails into fence posts. I don't want the bluebirds to abandon me. I don't want to mow trails. I don't want to eat dinner alone and avoid watching sunsets on the deck because it makes me sad. I don't want to live alone, but there's no one I want to live with except Vic. I don't want to be isolated. I don't want to deal with Vic's ninety-four-year-old mother who grieves over her only child and spews her resentment, as though I don't have enough of my own. I can't believe I rescued a vicious dog only to euthanize her and then bought a puppy that requires surgery, months of exercise restriction, and physical therapy.

Do I deserve this? Don't I deserve a break? The voice of reason breaks in to remind me of my good fortune. I ignore it.

I hate hoping things will get better rather than accepting things as they are. I hate that having a body means I will get sick. I hate that falling in love means the heart will be broken. I hate that being born means dying. I just hate.

Finally, because there is no one to pick up the pieces of my tantrum except me, I blow my nose, go inside, and focus the telescope on the new bluebird house.

∽ ∾

A few days later, a male bluebird sits on the roof. Tree swallows dive-bomb him. He leaves, returns, and leaves again. I don't see a female. She's the one who chooses where to live, so I expect she's chosen else-where. *After all I've done to make a perfect bluebird habitat and all I did to keep Vic alive, you'd think I would be treated better.* I will file a complaint with the Goddess of Bluebirds, but maybe it's smarter to be pissed at the environmental conservation guy for encouraging false hope.

Weeks later, a tardy bluebird couple claims the nesting box closest to the house rather than the new anger-contaminated box that sits fifty feet further away. I keep an eye on them through my binoculars. After the female warms and turns her eggs for at least a week, there is a rau-cous skirmish between the bluebirds and swallows that moved into the new box. The female bluebird attacks the swallows repeatedly and then sits on their box as they swoop and shriek in protest, but the swallows refuse to leave. Finally, the assailant returns to her house and ignores the swallows as she had before. Peace returns to the neighborhood.

Soon, the bluebird couple shuttles in worms and caterpillars and shuttles out mouthfuls of pale blue eggshell. I focus the telescope on the entryway to their house and watch, thrilled with every squirming larvae thrust through the nesting-box door toward the featherless fledg-lings hidden inside. Within days of the hatching, the parents' visits to the nest slow and then stop altogether. I wait three more days to make sure they're gone and investigate.

Unscrewing the front of the box, I dread the gore I might find inside, but there are no lively nestlings or tiny corpses inside. Instead, I find crushed straw swarming with frantic ants.

I walk back to the house to Google "bluebird predator ants." Sure enough, ants can invade a nest and kill baby birds. My gut cramps at the thought of ants biting the helpless naked bodies.

Following the website's directions, I scrub the inside of the box with hydrogen peroxide and rinse it repeatedly with water, leaving the front panel open to air and dry. I put drops of Terro, a low toxicity ant killer, into the deep crannies of the wood pole beneath the nesting box and smear an eight-inch barrier of Vaseline around the post. I hope the Vaseline will discourage the ants, but if it doesn't, the Terro will take care of them. I close the box and wait to see what happens next.

Within days, a beige and copper wren sits on the house where the murders took place. He spits out his exuberant staccato mating song, his chest lifted and his tail bobbing. He's late finding a home and mate, but he sings with confidence and hope. Through the telescope, I see sticks shifting inside the box, rearranged by a hidden housekeeper.

Despite catastrophe and repeated failures, new life persists and eventually takes flight. Even though the bluebirds lost everything, the female has a new nesting cavity by now and warms a new clutch of eggs. Birds do not understand hopelessness or failure. They keep trying.

Like other humans, I have favorite birds and preferred outcomes. Bluebirds have nested close to the house since Vic and I put up boxes about ten years ago. They reassure and comfort me with their shimmering beauty and industriousness during the best and hardest times. Drab little wrens are not as exciting as flashy sapphire and rusty-orange bluebirds who promised happiness in my childhood. I thought I could count on bluebirds, but must settle for less. Like wrens, my solitary life is plainer and less exciting than my old life, but still there is potential. Like the wrens and bluebirds, I will not give up hope.

Anthony's shoes are by the front door when I wake up. While he sleeps, I walk the dogs and make minestrone soup.

"How are things?" Anthony asks as we prepare lunch.

"Not much change since last time I saw you. Yesterday was our wedding anniversary. Challenging, but mostly I'm OK." Anthony puts his arm around me. We lean into each other for a few seconds and then he gets a square of paper towel, tears it in half, and hands me a piece. We both blow and wipe.

"How about you, Anthony?"

"Not much change." This isn't great, since Anthony longs for change.

"Is there any way I can help?"

"No, not really."

We eat big bowls of soup and go outside to do what we both love. We pull grasses and weeds out of the main flower bed, plant a few annuals, and fuss over flats of vegetables and flowers I bought earlier in the week. I watch for the indigo bunting I spotted yesterday, hoping to share his tropical blue beauty with Anthony.

Anthony inspects the vegetable garden and the beds we planted the last time he was here. He bends close to the earth to examine snow pea flowers and check the areas where the weeds got ahead of me.

"We'll tackle this tomorrow," he says. I know we will.

A few days later, David knocks on my bedroom door when he arrives from North Carolina around midnight. I get out of bed for hugs and sit on the pine floor in the kitchen in my pajamas, leaning against the cabinets, an arm around Willow. David and Anthony stand, leaning over the countertop while they drink cans of Guinness Draught. I relax beneath the energetic hum of my sons' energy, listening to them banter. They fish for mutual interests—the chores Anthony finished, the jobs left for David, the sharpness of the bush-hog blade, a mutual friend's marriage troubles.

"Grumpy and struggling, eh?" Anthony says mischievously, grinning down at me as he pushes my dream book to the edge of the counter.

It takes me a minute to connect. Then I realize I left my journal lying open on the kitchen counter after writing down a dream this morning. Anthony must have read the open pages during his ninety-minute phone call to United Airlines, negotiating with someone whose English wasn't up to the complexities of the ticket change Anthony wanted to make.

On hold for long stretches, he browsed whatever was on the counter, including my dream where I tell Vic his problem is adrenal stress. Dream Vic is grumpy about my New Age health ideas.

Next to the dream narrative, I had written what happened in my life yesterday: *Anthony is home, grumpy and struggling. We worked in the gardens and he cleared trails. I long for a dream about Vic since it's been a month since we last met in the night. Vic showed up, grumpy and resistant. Ha!!*

"Hey, you're not supposed to read my journal," I whine.

"Well, don't leave it open on the counter if you don't want me to read it," he teases. "Grumpy and struggling. I like it."

"Make it the title of your next record," David quips, his laughter arching over my head.

"Catchy," Anthony fires back. "Grumpy and Struggling."

"Dedicate it to me," I say with a grin.

I've been caught labeling my son's moody behavior, but he doesn't mind. I'm relieved his moodiness and my attempts to skirt around it are in the open. We're all moody these days.

In our family, grumpy and struggling means it's time to work. David and Anthony learned as kids that physical labor softens bad news, frustration, and disappointment. While Anthony worries about his music career, David figures out how to build his computer business, and I fret over finding a trail into my new life, we hoe and rake, weed and plant. The guys clear the trails of fallen branches and haul junk from the cellar for garbage day.

While we work, we talk about Vic and sometimes weep. These two men miss the same person I miss. We all feel stuck, but determined to make life hum again. New lives are emerging—chaotic and messy, grumpy and struggling.

In the morning, after Anthony leaves for New York City, David helps me pound in tomato stakes.

"Want to take a walk?" he asks when the stakes are in place.

We stroll along the freshly mowed trails past the lupine beds and pass new brush piles drying for fall burning and spring wildflower planting.

Willow and Daisy keep their noses close to the earth, quietly inhaling scents of the hidden creatures that live here. Willow walks close to me on leash. She is getting stronger and will soon run free, but our months of physical closeness and daily physical therapy have created a powerful bond. This time, my care has led to health rather than death.

From the main forest trail, we turn left to follow a side trail to the red oak knoll. David and I sit on round stones, making a triangle with Vic's cairn. Old Daisy is glad to lie down in the heat while Willow crunches last year's acorn caps. A woodpecker taps in the distance. A mourning dove coos—whooo, who, who. We speak quietly about the jobs completed during the brothers' overlapping visits and other tasks we will finish tomorrow.

"I'm sorry there's so much work to do, David."

"I like coming home, Mom, and I like working on this land."

Once again, I understand why I live here—a sixty-five-year-old woman in a too large house with a too large barn and too many gardens. I stay for the comfort this familiar place brings. David and Anthony were babies and teenagers here. They came to this forest and sat under these trees with their dad. They learned to use a chain saw and a cant hook and drank hot chocolate out of a Thermos on frigid firewood-cutting mornings. David loves his place in North Carolina and Anthony loves his San Francisco world, but this land is our mother and the Green Man lives here. For now, we need this home.

My father's doctors expected him to die before I was three. My mother was in a state of panic. Was I sad or afraid? Did I have tantrums? Years later, I questioned my mother and aunt.

"You were a good girl," they said, "obedient and cooperative. You rarely cried." It must have felt like a winning strategy, because Dad survived, weakened, but still on his feet.

On a dreary mid-November day in 1959, when I was fourteen, I went to my friend Carol's house after school. Mrs. Thomas, her proper white-aproned British mom, made us tea and toast with strawberry jam while my mother was at the hospital with dad.

Then the doorbell rang.

Mom and my brother Jim stood on the stoop, red-eyed and grim. I knew immediately that Dad was dead. I wanted them to go away. I wanted to take a bike ride or finish my homework. I wanted more toast and jam. I didn't want to go home.

Dutifully, I put on my jacket and grabbed my books. I sat in the back seat. No one spoke. Eighteen-year-old Jim drove, the man of the family now, with mom in the passenger seat. Beneath their silence, I heard an inner roar, like the sound of a wild wind ripping through leaves and breaking branches, the sound of destruction and the End of Days.

In a week, Jim returned to his freshman year at Yale, I returned to ninth grade, and mom, desperate to keep her new teaching job, returned to work. In the evening, mom disappeared into her bedroom, emerging to visit the refrigerator or bathroom, haggard with downcast eyes. My grandparents visited on weekends with cherry pie and tuna casserole. It was good to eat something besides TV dinners, but no one mentioned the obvious. Mom did not utter my father's name. If she surrendered to tears, she said, she couldn't grade her students' papers or get through her night school classes. Neither my mother nor I cried.

After dad's death, mom lived her life and let me live mine—as long as I got good grades and didn't get pregnant. Longing to see the world, she made plans to teach children of Air Force personnel at foreign bases while I was a freshman at Cornell. When she left for her first ten-month stay in Europe, I was seventeen. With no home base, no phone calls, and no parent, I sank into depression and struggled to get passing grades. I sat in my sixth-floor dorm room alone, reading Camus and crying myself into exhausted sleep.

When I was twenty-one, I was in love with Vic. As graduation neared, I wept about our coming separation. By the time I boarded a bus on the first leg of my trip to graduate school at Berkeley, Vic cried with me. I returned to Ithaca in two months, choosing love over graduate school. By then, emotional honesty was the ground of our relationship.

Vic rarely minded my tears. He said they told him what I valued. I cried at my wedding. I cried when our sons were born. I cried when my teacher Anthony died and when I saw the Dalai Lama. I cried when my sons left home. I cried when we learned that Vic's cancer was incurable. In our last two years together, Vic and I openly discussed our fears, our coming separation, and his death. There was plenty to cry about.

As Vic lay dying in the hospital, a friend suggested that my quiet bouts of weeping might disturb Vic's transition. It was important, the man said, not to hold Vic back. I told this man that Vic would worry about me if he didn't feel my warm tears on his hands.

"Hold me," Vic had asked two days before. "I feel like I'm going to sleep and won't wake up."

"That sounds like a good idea, Vic," I whispered in his ear. There was nothing ahead for his ravaged body except suffering. I did not cling. My tears were about letting go and saying good-bye.

Two years after Vic's death, I'm still crying. I cry not just for myself, but also for my friend who has cancer and for another friend in constant pain. I cry for a brave limbless soldier I read about in the *New York Times* and for the dolphins and birds dying in the oil spills in the Gulf of Mexico. Privately, my tears feel like teachers; but in front of others, I feel weak, out of control, and ashamed. I would like to hide my grief as mom and I once did, but I can't remember how.

"You're pregnant with grief," Lauren said soon after Vic died. "You're going through labor. A new life will come."

Preparing essays for Ellen Schmidt's weekly writing classes, I comb through my journals and memories and compose pieces dripping with sorrow. I rarely write about anything besides Vic's illness and death and the challenges of my new life without him. While I read my pieces out loud to the rest of the class, I weep. Each week Ellen gives me written and verbal feedback about my work, expressing her faith that within my torrent of grief, I am becoming a writer.

"You write with stunning honesty about your struggles," Ellen reassures me by email. "Your tears give others in the class permission and courage to write about their pain. Your stories, powered in strength from their vivid details, reveal the depth of your loss, the anger that surges in, the discouragement, and your very real triumphs and solid determination as well. Your compelling pieces inspire and strengthen others' work."

"Your tears give me permission to feel my own sorrow," Steve says.

I hear my friends, but still feel raw and exposed, even maudlin. Grief does not obey my will and stay out of sight. It will not go away.

Tears signal to people who don't know me that I'm falling apart and need to be saved. In fact, I am a strong woman with open feelings and wet eyes. Alongside my grief, a new life is being born. I cry, but there is still time to edit an essay for writing class, take Willow swimming in Seneca Lake, and make a pot of soup. When I stop criticizing myself, weeping becomes a sacred healing baptism, teaching me what I value.

Vic's death devastated and initiated me. I learned without doubt that life brings suffering and change is inescapable. I walked to the Gateway of Death and paused there. Then Vic went on without me. Standing at that threshold, I glimpsed my own mortality.

I can't see life singularly now. Life and death stand side by side, separated by only one inhalation.

8

Third year. Inner bonds sustain. Life takes root.

I sense an updraft, subtle, quiet, a whisper of wind. The downward pull of grief persists, but I often touch the slippery edge and rise above instead of being sucked under. After two years, I still miss meditating with Vic every evening and telling him my dreams each morning. I long for his touch, his laugh, and his loving gaze, but the sorrow rarely stops me in my tracks anymore.

Maybe the touch of lightness comes from living with a fully healed, bounding Willow. Maybe it's my growing involvement with Hospicare. Maybe it's the dream I had a few days ago that I'm moving my desk and books into a new, modern, well-lit room. My dream office is uncluttered with white walls and many windows, a space of new possibilities and light, new activities and images.

"What would you put on your bookcase?" my therapist asks.

"Bereavement, mythology, Jungian psychology, Buddhism, and health. Marion Woodman's books. Bird and plant identification books and my favorite memoirs. I want a philosophy section—Plotinus and Plato, Anthony Damiani and the Dalai Lama, Vic's three books—and a whole shelf for poetry." On top of my bookcase, I imagine an altar dedicated to the Sacred Feminine. I will decorate it according to the cycling of the seasons with summer gladiolas cut from my garden, crimson fall leaves, winter pinecones, and spring daffodils.

I still walk to the place where we buried Vic's ashes, refer to him when with friends, and weep over his absence, but his persistent inner presence brings more comfort and less pain. He is becoming part of me—an interior masculine energy constructed of the experiences, values, and love we shared. The outer Vic left in 2008, but the inner Vic evolves within. He is still my loving friend as I inch my way toward my new life.

Only days before Vic died, he whispered in his frail fierce voice, "I don't know what will happen to me, but I know that I will always love you."

Even as death broke down the door, his love was clear and strong. It still is. I am a woman blessed by love, and because of this, I'm doing just fine.

∽ ∾

I've longed for a grand project, something to make me more involved with the present and less involved with the irretrievable past. Last fall, a perfect possibility arrived on my doorstep, connecting back to when Vic and I bought our land in 1972 and linking to the future of this property when I'm gone.

In the autumn of 1971, Vic read me the property-for-sale ads in the *Ithaca Journal* and Schuyler County *Hi-Lites* while I nursed baby David. We hoped for something beautiful, affordable, and close to the meditation center we were helping to build on a piece of Anthony and Ella May Damiani's property near Seneca Lake. We inspected too many decrepit dark farmhouses with low ceilings, small rattling windows, inadequate heat, and brushy flat land, just because we could afford them.

In the spring of 1972, we found a perfectly located seventy-acre farm in the Town of Hector between Ithaca and the meditation center. The house, barn, and garage were a few years from collapse, while most of the motley sheds were beyond saving. I couldn't imagine living in this mess, but Vic looked it over with his engineer's eye and saw beyond the tarpaper siding and collapsing plaster. He focused on the straight roofline, salvageable foundation, plentiful clean water supply, and inspiring views. We arranged to return the next day for a tour of the land.

Driving back to our rented house on Cayuga Lake, Vic's eyes gleamed with unstoppable desire. He had always wanted land, and now he wanted this land.

The next day, the owner guided us through thirty-five acres of mature oak, maple, ash, hickory, beech, and evergreens, all in great condition compared to the house. The household dumps, rusted car bodies, and mountain of abandoned tires would require a grueling cleanup. The messes frightened and overwhelmed me, but the shadbush trees shimmered with tiny white flowers in the hedgerows and yellow trout lilies glowed near eager streams.

Vic salivated. I worried.

Climbing the hill behind the house, we turned toward the southwest and watched deer grazing in the field below us, framed by an apricot and lavender "Good God Almighty" sunset blasting across the horizon. The following day, we made a purchase offer of $11,800 for the seventy acres and buildings, despite our concern about the two acres that had been chopped out of the property for the owner's parents' trailer an eighth of a mile down the road. By then, we knew that any piece of property we could afford came with drawbacks.

I was a small-town girl, although I stalked cattails and burdock roots with Euell Gibbons and cooked whole wheat molasses cookies with Adele Davis. I wanted a garden and I loved the views, but the windows crumbled with rot and peeling pieces of plywood covered missing panes. The wooden siding on the north side of the house hadn't seen paint since God knows when, while flapping faded tarpaper covered the rest of the place. The inside looked like a set for a depression era movie—dimly lit and dirty with cracked worn linoleum in patterns vaguely reminiscent of Oriental rugs, all glued and nailed to unfinished pine floors. Sheets of plastic covered the insides of windows, providing all I needed to know about indoor winter temperatures.

No matter. Vic was smitten.

"It has a new furnace and the springwater is delicious. It has electric and telephone, and the road is quiet. We'll save this old girl," he promised.

Vic knew how to use a hammer and skill saw. I had seen him shingle roofs, plumb a toilet, and hang windows. He wasn't frightened by the broken and rotting and we both knew how to work hard, so I trusted that somehow we would make this place right.

We moved in on July 1, 1972, carrying our boxes beneath the fragrant blossoms of the horse chestnut in the front yard and the buzzing hum of bumblebees drunk with nectar. By the end of the summer, we covered the rough walls of the kitchen and living room with bright paint and traded storm windows for the sheets of plastic. I learned how to glaze windows and replaced each of the twelve panes in all twenty-two windows. Vic tackled the roof and ripped the plywood off the back porch where the previous owners raised rabbits. That first winter, two-year-old David received his first lessons in dressing in layers, as I hurriedly changed his diapers on a blanket on the floor near the old Franklin stove. Together we huddled for warmth with our cat, our first Labrador retriever puppy, and racks of drying diapers.

In 1973, only a year after we'd moved into our dream house, Vic landed a job teaching physics and astronomy at Colgate University in Hamilton, New York, a hundred miles away from our new land and the meditation center. The job was too good to pass up, so we kept our Hector home and rented a small place near Colgate where we stayed while classes were in session. Hamilton was the work camp. Hector was home.

In 2005, Vic and I signed a conservation easement with the Finger Lakes Land Trust. After watching a greedy lumber company decimate a neighboring forest, oak by oak, we wanted to protect our forest from such a fate. Our property was still privately owned, but would remain undeveloped and undivided with a management plan to keep the fields, forest, and wetlands healthy. The conservation easement allowed us to love each tree and stream, knowing the land would be protected after our deaths.

Vic and I continued fretting over the separated acres down the road, the missing edge piece of our favorite jigsaw puzzle. There were two trailers on those acres now. The second was an attractive residence set back from the road and hidden from our view by a tall spruce hedge; but the closest trailer was vacant, rusted, and surrounded by dust-bowl style outbuildings, all starkly visible from the best sunset-viewing spot above our house.

Last summer, a For Sale sign appeared in front of the vacant trailer, but without Vic, it seemed foolish to take on more property and responsibility.

"You have to buy that place," David insisted, predictably channeling Vic's point of view.

"You've been lucky and had old people or no one living there," Anthony argued. "You don't know who might move in."

They were right. There is no zoning in the Town of Hector. I could live next to the constant bang-bang-bang of a neighbor practicing his aim for hunting season or the stench of a turkey farm. There could be a go-cart track or a used car lot. The only way to protect my home and view was to buy the acre.

The last day of September 2009, I went to the lawyer to sign the deed. When he asked for my social security number, I wrote down Vic's instead of my own. I dammed my tears, keeping myself rational enough to read what I had to sign. I got through the paperwork and walked away feeling nothing. No joy, no sense of accomplishment, no victory. What was the use without Vic here to celebrate with me?

I left the trailer vacant last winter. I hoped to give it to someone who would haul it off, but learned it is illegal in New York State to move an old trailer and set it up as a residence elsewhere. I checked into hauling the trailer to a landfill, but found no practical solution for recycling or dumping the monster off site. Last winter as I walked the trails, I decided there was only one way forward—tear the trailer down along with the dilapidated buildings around it and bury everything. I was assured that nothing would be left in the trailer to pollute the groundwater. I hoped this was true.

A trusted man came with his sons, backhoe, and bulldozer. They stripped the trailer of what could be reused and recycled, dug a mammoth hole, bulldozed the trailer and the buildings into the earth, and covered them with a thick layer of soil. When they were done, I stood at the top of the hill above my home with Willow and watched the sunset. I admired the expanse of open land down the hill and imagined the willows and spruce trees I would plant to begin reforestation.

Today, I saw the lawyer again and began the process of protecting this acre from development. I plan to merge the properties and amend the agreement with the Finger Lakes Land Trust to include the new parcel in the conservation easement.

You might think that mending the land binds me more strongly to it, but instead it releases me. This land supported my family for thirty-seven years, and it will be here long after I'm gone. Like the first owner, Ebenezer Jewell in 1805, and like Vic, I am only a caretaker. Like everything else in life, that job is temporary. When I walk or am carried away from this place, I will leave knowing the land is whole and the wildlife and forest are safe. I do it for Vic and the land, but also to mend myself.

Rain hammers the car as I drive toward Rochester in the August thunderstorm. Truck tires hurl buckets of water on the windshield. The wipers slap back and forth, but I can't drive over forty miles per hour and I'm going to be late for my appointment. *Democracy Now* blares on the radio, lamenting the BP oil spill in the Gulf of Mexico and the growing negativity toward Obama who is expected to magically heal every crisis he inherited.

I am anxious about my hearing and distract myself by thinking of more catastrophic issues. I've progressively lost hearing since 1998. Nothing stopped my growing deafness, not acupuncture, not chiropractic, not homeopathy, not healing sessions, certainly not fancy medical testing.

Going deaf was manageable when I was married to someone who was willing to yell when necessary and plant himself in front of me so I could read his lips. I called Vic from the parking lot after each annual visit to Strong Audiology in Rochester as my hearing grew weaker and the hearing aids grew stronger.

"We'll deal with this," Vic assured me. When I got home, he silently drew the outline of a Valentine on his chest and pointed repeatedly from his heart to mine with a few theatrical winks. He loved me, deaf or not.

One-on-one or in a group where people speak one at a time, I manage with the help of hearing aids and lip reading. If the acoustics are poor or there is background noise, I'm lost and isolated. It's hard to make new friends when restaurant clatter muddles my hearing and music grates. A bad cell phone connection sounds muddy and incomprehensible.

Today, I'm working myself into a tension headache. I don't have much hearing left to lose, especially in my right ear.

I relax when I'm in Dr. Matt MacDonald's office. He's a handsome man in his forties with an open-hearted smile. Photos of family cover the cabinets.

"How are you doing on your own?" he asks as he ushers me into the soundproof testing booth.

"It's easier than it was," I tell him. I want to add that I'm apprehensive about my hearing, but he knows that.

His gentle touch reassures me as he places the headphones over my ears. Then he leaves me in the booth, sits on the other side of a window of glass, and speaks to me through headphones. He asks me to hold up my hand when I hear a tone. Halfway through the test, he flashes a grin. When we've gone through all the steps, he beams.

"Your hearing hasn't changed in the last two years," Matt tells me. "Actually, it hasn't changed in four years and your hearing aids don't need adjusting. I'm hopeful that the loss has plateaued." He looks through my records again and checks old tests.

"The most interesting thing," he continues, "is that your word comprehension went from 56 percent to 88 percent in your worst ear. I don't get it, but it's terrific."

"The last time you checked my word comprehension was two years ago," I remind him, "a few weeks after Vic's death. I spent most of my time crying then. My ears were full of tears. Maybe now I'm ready to hear the words of my new story."

On a hot July night, David drives me to Grass Roots in Trumansburg, about ten miles from home. The Grass Roots Festival of Music and Dance is a big deal in my neighborhood and a national destination for the folk music world. Vic and I enjoyed spending a few evenings at the bacchanal, pretending we were back in the sixties, but I haven't been to Grass Roots for many years. Anthony, a San Francisco techno DJ, will play music in a long low-roofed building called the Cabaret sometime between one and four a.m. Those hours are a big stretch for a woman who rarely stays up past eleven, but I haven't heard Anthony play in five years—partly because of Vic's illness and partly because of the hours Anthony keeps.

David and Anthony don't come home as often as they did two years ago. I don't need as much help on the property because I count on Matt Hoff, a young woodsman Vic found to help with firewood and mowing. Matt knows how to run a chain saw, read and follow a tractor maintenance manual, and manage the property. He loves the forest as much as I do. I also don't need my sons as much emotionally, so this is the first time the three of us have been together since Christmas.

David and I search through the crowd clustered under the dance tent until we find Steve and Janet. David arranges to meet Steve and me at the Cabaret at one a.m. before leaving to find his brother. I dance with Janet, trying not to think about the forty years I danced with Vic.

Steve and I get to the Cabaret a little late. The volume hurts, so I take out my hearing aids and stuff earplugs in my ears.

"I need these," Anthony had said as he placed a set of earplugs in my hand after dinner. "So do you."

The music has a heavy beat, a little like hip-hop, a little like rap, a lot like disco. Anthony calls himself a DJ, but my 1960s idea of a guy who plays records is miles away from what he does. He creates music with a keyboard, synthesizers, turntables, and sound bites—dance music, "house" music, stay-up-all-night music, welcome-the-sunrise music. He creates music on vinyl for other DJs and puts out CDs. Anthony plays at music festivals, in nightclubs and cafés, and at Burning Man in the desert.

Anthony rocks the room of a few hundred dancers. At the back of the crowd, David helps me climb up on the seat of a wooden chair against a wall. My friend Barbara joins us, sleepy-eyed and out of place like me. Above the bouncing crowd of Dionysian dancers, Anthony stands on stage. I watch his agile hands from my perch. I sway to the music. David guards me with his strong body so I don't get knocked off the chair.

In this open space with a big dance floor and decent sound system, Anthony shines for the hometown crowd. I'm happy feeling the sturdy love my sons and I have for each other as we rejoice in each other's good fortune and support each other in sorrow.

∽ ≫

In the fall of 2010, I look over the 140 pieces I've written in Ellen Schmidt's writing classes and wonder if I have the bones of a book.

"After one and a half years of steady writing, you have a body of work," Ellen told me. "You have the makings of a memoir," she said, acknowledging what I'm afraid to notice. I also have detailed journals to help me fill in the blank spots, but I've never written anything longer than ten pages. I'm not sure I have the guts to pull this off.

With this idea simmering, I dream of Vic wearing a motorcycle helmet and full-body leathers. His hands firmly grasp the handlebars of a small motorcycle. His bearded face tenses with concentration. He runs alongside the accelerating motorcycle as he prepares to leap on, just as a bareback rider catapults his body to mount a moving horse.

In 1967, I took a photo of Vic running beside his motorcycle at a racetrack in Canada. He raced a small Spanish-made motorcycle, a nimble little red machine that was not as powerful as the larger motorcycles he raced against. Vic made up for lost time in the straightaway by laying the bike down low in the turns and flying fast as the wind. The crew pit where Vic incessantly tuned his bike reeked of gasoline, 2-cycle engine oil, and sweaty leather. The roaring machines flew past in a blur of chrome and exhaust fumes. They thrilled and terrified me. Each time Vic began a race, I watched in horror as he rounded the first turn and disappeared from view. I held my breath and waited for him to come around the track before he disappeared again.

Now, forty-two years later, this particular Vic shows up in my dream world. Not sick Vic or dead Vic or sad Vic or lover Vic, the usual visitors in my dreams. Not professor or spiritual seeker or writer Vic, but a wild, testosterone-driven warrior from the first months of our relationship. Vic gave up racing soon after we met and motorcycle Vic transformed into a woodsman and builder after we bought our home. The passionate vitality of a red-bearded daredevil remained.

I first met Vic in a motorcycle shop at the corner of State and Corn streets in Ithaca in 1966. He had short black hair, a muscular body, and wore full-body coveralls. He leaned over an upside down motorcycle skeleton with a wrench in his hand. Even before we were introduced, I thought: I want to marry that man. A rush of inner heat filled my body and left no room for doubt. As our relationship unfolded, I let Vic take the role of warrior in our world.

I explore the dream images with Robert Bosnak and other participants in this year's annual workshop. I experience Vic's competence, daring, and concentration in my hands and forearms. I feel the strong grip and taut muscles in my arms and shoulders and the thrill and focus of a dangerous challenge.

A few days later, I review the dream with my therapist who helps me dig out memories and associations. What did I first notice about Vic in 1966? What unconscious part of myself did I recognize in him? What part of me runs alongside a moving vehicle and dares to take a leap?

Dream Vic leans forward, focused on the task ahead, unconcerned with success or failure, giving it all he has. If a racer doesn't vault his body onto the accelerating machine and take control, he and his bike will be run over by other motorcycles and destroyed. Once the racer is committed, there is no backing out.

These warrior powers were Vic's throughout his life and in his final fight, but he wasn't the only one carrying these qualities. I also have a strong weightlifter's grip and a courageous heart. I am fierce, focused, and daring when cornered. The woman who stood on the helicopter pad and refused to follow the orders of the men in white coats is still here. I know how to stand my ground and take a leap.

My cautious self wants to wait safely on the sidelines rather than begin an overwhelming book project, but another part of me knows that it's time to grab the reins, the horns, and the handlebars and write my book. My vehicle is in first gear, revving with anticipation. There is momentum in my life, and it's dangerous to let it stall.

Marion Woodman writes twice after I send her the dream and my thoughts about it. I've corresponded with her since 2003, drinking in her encouragement and faith. The pace of our correspondence accelerated when Vic became ill and quickened again after his death.

Six weeks after Vic's death, Marion soothed me with maternal words, "How I wish I could hold you in my arms and be silent together. I know how close you and Victor were." A year later, she wrote, "Something is emerging that could not have happened in your old life. It will come through."

After receiving my letter, Marion writes: "Healing happens. I know where you are. Believe it. Just act. DO IT. Launch yourself—use the warrior energy to create your own new life." In February 2011, she writes for the last time. "Be gentle with yourself. Let the warm love flow." I soon learn that she is ill and housebound, no longer able to teach and, I assume, no longer able to write. I will have to internalize Marion as my Wise Woman, just as I'm internalizing Vic as my Masculine Warrior.

Lourdes forwards an email she received from Vic a few years ago.

"I was reading a transcript of an interview with Marie-Louise von Franz, very near the end of her life," Vic wrote. "She is asked, 'What is the place of individuation in a love relationship?'"

> In a love relation, you risk everything. You put yourself on the table, you stop the power games and trying to dominate or conquer the other person. If you succeed in really loving the other person, if you really relate, then all sorts of miracles happen.[18]

Marie Louise von Franz was an early student of Carl Jung, a psychotherapist, and a prolific writer. After I read Lourdes' email, I take von Franz's book *Psychotherapy* from my bookshelf. Leafing through her discussion of the psychological functions, I see a note in Vic's handwriting in the margin. "When Elaine left for CA in 1967, I was numb. It took me months to realize how much I loved her."

Vic and I risked everything for love and put everything on the table. Our love went beneath and around the power games that arose; it was unthreatened by anger or unavoidable failures. Our love was unthreatened even by death. We compromised, complained, forgave, and laughingly called each other worthy adversaries.

"What's your daddy like?" a stranger asked our son David when he was three years old.

"My daddy's tough as nails."

"What's your momma like?" the woman asked.

"My momma talks back."

Remembering through the lens of love, it's easy to forget the hard parts of our marriage, but I was sometimes jealous of Vic's position in the world. Vic didn't resent the compromises he'd made for marriage. I told him with a jab of my smart tongue that our marriage gave him nothing to be angry about. A year after his death, I found a journal entry Vic wrote long before his illness: "E will soon return from town and disturb my peace with bitchy complaints." I laughed and then felt remorse for my nasty side. I wish I had softened that edge. Too late for that now.

It's hard to stomach the finality of "too late for that now." This morning, before meditation, I took my wedding ring from my altar and slipped it on my right ring finger. I hadn't worn the ring for a year. It felt good on my hand, and I wore it for a half hour of silent sitting. *This is my wedding ring no matter what hand it's on. I am no longer married to Vic in this life; I am on my own and need to take advantage of that.* I took the ring off and put it back on my altar.

But the longing for Vic and our life persists. I carry the ache of grief through breakfast. It lifts when I dress the dogs in their orange hunting-season capes and put on my orange vest. Who can be sad on an autumn day of golden sunlight and bronze leaves? The cosmos still bloom with pink exuberance. I pick a few to place on the flat shale slab at Vic's cairn.

As I walk, I remember an incident soon after Vic's stem cell transplant when we invited friends over. The long hospitalization and procedure had been grueling and frightening. Of course, it was hardest for Vic, but after an hour of hearing him tell his story, my jaws locked and my head smoked.

"You're only interested in Vic and not in me," I hissed, shocking our friends and myself. How could I insist on sharing the stage with a stem-cell transplant survivor? I wasn't the one who was physically demolished and confined without the solace of nature. I wasn't the one with cancer. Still, I was with Vic every step of the way. I had my own difficult experience and wanted to tell it, but our friends focused on

Vic and he had plenty to say. My anger hurt Vic, but he understood my need to tell the story from my side.

Vic and I didn't have major disagreements about the way we raised our sons or which spiritual path to follow, or even minor ones about what we wanted for dinner. Our problems focused on one issue. Vic loved the spotlight. I sometimes felt lost in his shadow.

Our balance of power was equal in most ways. We made decisions together and when we disagreed, we both had veto power. He made money, while I managed and invested it. He cut the trails and firewood and stacked the dried wood on the front porch. I was the vegetable gardener and bought the groceries. I was the chef. He was the prep cook and dishwasher. For the most part, we lived in harmony.

I edited his articles and books, gave honest feedback, and helped make his writing accessible to nonscientists. I rejoiced with him when a book was accepted for publication. He thanked me profusely, privately and publicly. He also edited my writing, but I rarely submitted anything for publication. Instead, I felt cheated when my efforts supported his success but couldn't seem to support my own. This wasn't Vic's fault, but I needed to blame someone.

In truth, I was the one who decided to have babies rather than go to graduate school. I was the one who preferred to be the support person at home when our sons were young. Vic backed me completely when I returned to school to get a nutrition degree and years later when I became a personal trainer.

During his illness, my unresolved competition fell into the background, but it never entirely disappeared. Now I need to look clearly at the compromises I made for love. In this new life, I look squarely at paths not taken. There is still time for neglected possibilities. I can no longer blame Vic.

For the past year, I've talked to my friend Barbara daily as she and her husband Richard navigate his cancer therapy. It reassures her to report experiences to a friend who has been in a chemotherapy room and waited anxiously for test results. I'm happy to hold her hand through this, just as she supported me during Vic's illness.

In the spring of 2008, she and Richard drove to Strong Hospital to spend the day with us. Vic was hospitalized for another round of alarming heart symptoms mysteriously related to lymphoma. Richard read Vic to sleep with poetry and then sat silently with him in the darkened hospital room. Barbara and I found a bright corner near a wall of windows in the hospital dining room, spread watercolor paper out on a formica-topped table, and painted.

Barbara is an artist and teacher. She knows that playing with color soothes anguish. Using bright acrylics, I painted a muscular grey horse from Rilke's *Sonnets to Orpheus.* Vic needed animal vitality. So did I.

Since Richard's diagnosis with cancer in January of 2010, I've learned that I can be with friends in crisis without dissolving in my own grief. Usually, I can step out of my own story and help others stand in theirs. I also feel at home at Hospicare. A few of my articles have been published on their website and I want to be more involved, so I sign up for a twenty-hour volunteer training in October. Within a few months, I take bereavement training, too, imagining the possibility of leading bereavement groups for women who have lost spouses or partners.

What if I cry while I lead a group? What if my emotions spill out?

As long as I focus on the experience of the person I'm with, my grief won't get in the way. Barbara teaches me that.

In late November, I drive home from North Carolina on familiar roads and get lost three times—once by turning too soon, twice by driving past my exit. Maybe I'm distracted by listening to a CD, but the real issue is I'm on my way home, a transition that grabs me by the throat and throws me to the ground.

I pull in the driveway at 5:10 p.m. in fog and drizzle. The dogs need to be fed and walked after a long day in the car. I pull on my rain pants and hiking boots and walk down the main trail. There is enough light to see the ground beneath my feet and make out the hedgerow, but not enough to be captivated by the comfortable familiarity of these fields. Instead, I'm isolated in fog, sinking into a pit of loneliness. Vic is not here in the place where I still expect to find him. Instead, I feel the presence of his absence, a deep aching emptiness in the pit of my stomach and a constriction around my heart. He is not here, and he will not be here.

In his book *Loving Grief*, Paul Bennett points out a truth that keeps me afloat: Grief is none other than the love we feel for the person who is gone. Grief is the way my love feels now. *This longing is my love. This pain is my love.* The words ride on my breath like a mantra, opening and softening my chest.

I listened to mindfulness lectures on CDs during my drive home. Pema Chodron reminds me to be curious instead of anxious. She reminds me to wait and watch rather than assuming the worst. She reminds me that I am not alone in grief. Hundreds and thousands and millions of others feel a similar aching emptiness at this very moment. Everyone hurts. Everyone suffers loss. My situation is not unique or special. It's human.

续 ﻪ

The next day, editing a story about my early married years when death felt far away, the heartache persists despite morning sunshine. Outside with the dogs, I pick four crimson apples from the weeping crabapple tree in the yard and carry them with me to the woods. I lay these bright orbs on the stones at Vic's place—red exuberance against gray shale. I wonder if a creature of the woods will enjoy them tonight.

Walking later that evening, after a long autumn sunset, I admire the crescent moon and the brightness of Jupiter, but can't escape my misery. Near the stream, a moan escapes from my chest. Willow comes running, distracted from her sniffing exploration, but when she understands I'm not calling her, she returns to her search. Daisy stays close by. In desperation, I tip my head back and howl at the sky. I weep and yip at the moon hanging low in the west. There is no answer for my anguish, but my belly and chest let go and the beauty and serenity of the land rush in to fill the open space.

❧ ❧

Anthony showed up at around three last night, December 20. This morning, he wakes up groggy-eyed, makes a pot of coffee, and takes a run. He doesn't have much to say, so I let my words rest. He leads an extroverted life—all promotion, all the time—and relishes the quiet of his childhood home. He is the son who spent hours playing alone with Legos or GI Joes in his bedroom as a child. While David couldn't get enough interaction, Anthony cherished his quiet inner spaces.

After lunch, Anthony is ready to talk. He knows I want to hear about his life, so he accommodates. I appreciate his generosity and tell him about life on the land, about the dogs, and about writing. We share the joys and struggles of creative work.

"I used to think my next single or CD would make me famous, but I let that go," he confides. "I'm happy to be going to Japan to play, and I'm happy when I release new music." Wise thoughts for me to contemplate as a writer.

"It's six o'clock," Anthony reminds me while we're making dinner. "Solstice is at six-thirty."

"Want to light candles?" I ask.

"Sure," Anthony agrees.

I spread a small red cloth on the tabletop I cleared earlier in the day. At six-thirty we light candles, wish each other a Blessed Solstice, and agree to do something more elaborate when David arrives tomorrow. Since Solstice is a pause more than a point in time, I like spreading our ritual over a few days.

The next morning, I take pruning shears and a cloth bag on my morning hike and gather spruce and pine boughs and three types of pinecones. I put a few small slabs of shale in my bag and two chunks of granite. After lunch, I empty my bag on the dining room table, put a favorite photo of Vic next to the cones, and wait to see what will happen.

"What are we going to do with this stuff?" David asks around dusk as he paws through my forest treasure.

"I thought you guys might build an altar with me, maybe light a few candles with the intention of letting something end and something new begin." I feel tentative and shy, defending myself from getting shot down by my sons.

"Great. Let's do it," David says with enthusiasm. He picks up a red pine branch and puts it behind the two candles Anthony and I lit last night. I put a spruce bough on one side of the candles, and Anthony puts a white pine branch on the other. We put more candles around the greens, add stones, and scatter pinecones in little clusters.

"And this?" David asks, picking up the photo of Vic as the Green Man with his face surrounded by red maple leaves.

"Well, I thought I'd put it in the back," I say quietly, "slightly hidden beneath the evergreens so you have to pay attention to notice it, Green Man style. Is that OK with you?"

"Of course," they say. I tuck the photo behind the red pine boughs. Vic's eyes gaze out at the three of us through the greens; our fourth watching from the other side.

"Let's say what we want to release and what we hope for this coming year," I suggest. "Or you could just light a candle. You don't have to say anything."

Anthony goes first, silently lighting a candle and wiping tears with his shirt sleeve. David goes next, describing in detail what he wants to leave behind and what he wants to add to his life before lighting his candle. Anthony thinks better of his silence and speaks his heart's desire while he lights a second candle.

"It's your turn, Mom," Anthony says.

"Fewer tears. More joy," I pray.

Epilogue

I gather pine and spruce cones, evergreen branches, stones from the stream, and feathers from my forest. I lay a red cloth on a cabinet and put my favorite photo of Vic at the back. This year, since my sons won't be here at the same time to observe the winter solstice, there will be two rituals: one with Anthony and another a few days later with David and Liz.

David married Liz in June of 2013. She is a dark-haired beauty who brings love, support, and laughter to our family, so we are four again. I call her the answer to my solstice prayers. Two days before her June wedding, she helped our family create a simple ritual of remembrance to mark the fifth anniversary of Vic's death. Lauren and Steve came to the wedding early to be part of our ritual. Liz's parents and another close friend also joined us.

We sat on David and Liz's back porch in the soft evening light, made a simple altar with Vic's photo and a few flowers and stones. Liz read "The Lord is my shepherd. Yea, though I walk through the valley of the shadow of death, I shall fear no evil." Lauren read Naomi Shihab Nye's poem "Kindness." David and Anthony said a few quiet words about loving and missing their dad. Steve told stories about meeting Vic as a student at Colgate. I recited a poem Naomi had sent by email a few days earlier. The words circled in my head like a mantra, a prayer, the truth: "People do not/ pass away/ They die/ and then/ they stay."

We ended by singing "Let It Be" with a larger circle of voices than when David, Anthony, and I sang those words in the woods after burying Vic's ashes. With tears, hugs, poems, and prayers, we created a space for our grief. Afterward, we could turn our hearts to celebration.

David and Liz married under the outspreading branches of "Vic's Tree" at their home in North Carolina. Vic admired this ancient oak, sat under it, and photographed it, so David named it after his dad. Liz offered her bouquet to Vic's Tree after the wedding ritual. Friends and family joined us from California, New York, and Massachusetts for a sunny North Carolina day. It felt right to wear my wedding ring for my son's wedding, so I slipped it on my left finger for just that day, keenly aware of Vic's absence and his presence. And then I danced and laughed and danced some more.

❦ ❧

Political protest and environmental activism were always part of life with Vic. In 1966 and 1967, Vic and I cemented our love and common political values by burning draft cards at Cornell and working on political causes on campus. We went to anti-Vietnam War rallies in Buffalo, New York City, and Washington—snuggling under a blanket in the bus on the way home, caressing each other in the dark.

In 2001, Vic and I protested gas drilling in the National Forest bordering our land. Along with many others, we won that battle.

Now I'm a member of Gas Free Seneca and Earth Vigil and work to stop fracking in New York State. I focus on stopping the gas industry from storing liquid petroleum gas in the salt mines beneath Seneca Lake. The nuclear industry proposed spent fuel-rod storage in the mines some years back, but the permit was denied because of fault lines under the caverns. Apparently, LP gas under the lake and a plan to turn this exquisite tourist area into the LP gas distribution center for the northeastern United States doesn't evoke the same fears as nuclear waste.

I labored for many days over a four-page comment letter to the New York Department of Environmental Conservation to protest the gas company's plan. I focused on every alarming problem with the proposed storage site including a fourteen-acre brine pond, a sixty-foot flare stack, and a noisy industrial facility. There are nearly a hundred salt mines nearby. The possibilities are alarming.

I don't want to be angry and bitter about the threat to my area, so I often drive three miles from my home to the shore of Seneca Lake in the evening. The water mirrors the setting sun and apricot streaked sky. Willow, who takes to the water like a harbor seal, bounces and quivers with anticipation. I walk to the end of the boat launch dock and hurl a stick. Willow launches her sleek brown body off the dock, belly flops with a splat, and pumps toward the stick. My tight shoulders drop with a sigh. I see how my anger mirrors the antagonism of the gas company that feels thwarted by protesters. Anger closes my heart and makes me forget that we are on this planet together, living and dying together.

I turn to what has helped me survive many hostile town and county government meetings and chant an ancient name of the lake as a healing prayer for Her and for myself. *Ga nun da sa ga Te car ne o di.* A local conservation forester, whose grandmother was a Seneca Indian clan mother, told me the lake loves hearing Her true Indian name. When I repeat the sounds inwardly or out loud, my heart opens and I remember to hold a calm center in the midst of frustration, betrayal, and human greed for cheap energy.

Mother Seneca soothes my anger with her placid water. I feel her calm acceptance of what is. She will be here long after these unruly gas companies, this town, and I are gone. I pray we will leave Seneca clean and full of life for those who come after us.

I also attend fracking protests in Albany and on a bitter winter day went to Washington, D.C., for the Forward on Climate Rally to protest the Keystone XL Tar Sands Pipeline. The rally was supported by 168 environmental groups, from the Sierra Club and 350.org to Indigenous Environmental Network, Hip Hop Caucus, and New Yorkers Against

Fracking. People of many colors huddled together on the stage, some wrapped in bright Navajo blankets to protect themselves from the wind. I was deeply moved by the Native American women who spoke on behalf of Earth and their people, their children and all children.

I joined the last eight miles of a Prayer Walk around Seneca Lake organized by a local activist and an Ojibwa woman elder called the Mississippi River Walker. My legs ached and a blister throbbed, but I didn't slow down. I focused on the copper vessel ahead of me with its beaded red cloth cover. It held sacred water collected four days earlier at the southern lake shore and was carried by a relay of walkers eighty miles around the lake. A woman carried the vessel, always a woman. A man or woman carried an eagle feather for protection of the water. When it was my turn to carry the water, I felt honored, quiet, and filled with hope. I knew it was my sacred duty to help protect this lake and Earth.

Mixing political protests with spirituality feels most natural to me. The Dalai Lama's emphasis on protecting the Earth and environment inspires me to combine my spiritual practice and environmental concerns, so I meditate often with Earth Vigil from the Rochester Zen Center at the gates of the planned, although not yet approved, LPG facility on Seneca Lake.

∸ ∽

After hospice volunteer bereavement training, I hoped to offer comfort and support to others who grieve. My skills from leading women's health classes became part of my life again when I was asked to lead support groups for women who have lost spouses or partners. I named my group "Standing in Our New Lives" from the last image of the poem "Oceans" that begins this book. Unfortunately, there is an endless supply of new widows, but now our hospice has a specific support group just for them. My classes include poetry, telling our stories, discussion, problem-solving without giving advice, and simple rituals such as writing our prayers and hopes for our new life on small pieces of paper. Some women bury, compost, or burn them. Others keep them in special places in their homes, often next to a picture of the person they miss. I am honored to meet these women and feel an immediate intimacy and bond because of our common loss.

I also write for the Hospicare website, online newsletter, and bereavement newsletter and make phone calls to people who have lost partners. Bereavement work is my calling, my vocation, and my passion.

My small garden with an abundance of weeds still provides plenty of food for me and my mother-in-law. I make salads and nourishing soups and share them with those who need support, especially dear friends from the Wisdom's Goldenrod community. I feel closer than ever to the women in the mythology group and we continue to work on new cultural myths and learn about the Sacred Feminine.

My dog Daisy, the friend who stood at my side through Vic's illness and after his death, died quietly of old age. Willow curls up on her dog bed as I write, waiting for our next walk.

Vic still visits in dreams, but with less intensity now. Inwardly, he is always with me, in some ways more strongly than just after his death. Now he is a constant heart presence. He is my inner husband, as long as my attachment doesn't stop me from living—and it doesn't. Instead, his closeness makes me live with more courage, joy, and curiosity. I once apologized for my continuing relationship with Vic since our culture thinks those who grieve should move on and get over it, but my bond with Vic is a gift. I build my new life on the supportive foundation we created and the person I became during our life together.

Of course, I long to watch for bluebirds with Vic and hold his warm hand in the woods rather than leaving flowers at the place where his ashes are buried. But I have grown and changed in ways that wouldn't have happened if he were still alive. I'm more self-confident and get less upset about the small stuff. My daily spiritual practice continues to be meditation, kindness, and the search for beauty and love wherever I find it. I do not forget how fragile this life is. I don't make excuses when I'm afraid of the next step. And instead of supporting Vic's writing and career, I support my own creative work.

The beauty of our land still heals and comforts me. I occasionally go to dream workshops or visit spiritual teachers, but solitude is my most powerful teacher and the forest is my sanctuary. I'm not ready to leave here. I keep the trails cleared, fields mowed, and firewood on the porch because Vic hired Matt Hoff to help us before he died. Matt and his wife and daughters are part of my large circle of support. Matt calls himself my land steward. I joke that I must be the Duchess.

Grief doesn't end for me, or anyone. If we dare to love, then we will grieve. Mortality is the shadow that falls when the sun shines. Life doesn't stop reminding me. My mother-in-law falls. My friend's son dies for no known reason. After a hard battle with cancer, the wife of another friend dies and I have more friends with grave illnesses. I hold them in their struggles just as they held me. I make soup and phone calls and reserve a space in my heart for those who grieve. I weep, but not as much for myself and Vic. I weep for the suffering of those I love and for the struggling Earth, for the beauty of a golden sunset or whitecaps rippling across Seneca Lake.

Vic's death taught me that only kindness and love matter in the end. When we fall, and we all will fall, we can rise up if we lean into each other and the sacred gift of life.

May we all learn to lean into love.

Acknowledgments

Thanks to my loving sons David and Anthony who stood by their dad and me through the best and worst. I'm grateful to David's wife Liz who brought new joy and love to our family.

Thank you, Steve Smolen and Lauren Cottrell Banner, who said, "We'll stay with you until the end." They did not leave my side. I'm grateful for the women in my mythology class who held me in love and helped me find a place to stand in the cycle of illness, death, and renewal.

As Vic's dream foretold, our community created a healing cocoon woven of herbs and silver threads. I'm grateful to those who talked to me on the phone late at night during the worst times and willingly witnessed my grief, to Cindy Stillman who cared for my dog for weeks at a time, and to family and friends who visited, made soup, and sent flowers. Thank you to those who kept Vic's mother company during Vic's last days. Thank you to friends, close and far away, who read Vic's emails and sent him love and poems.

I will never forget those who gathered to meditate on the floor in the Cayuga Medical intensive care room and made a circle of protective love around Vic and me. You came to my rescue before I knew how much I needed you. Thank you to those who came to Rochester during Vic's last days, read poetry and inspired words, prayed for quiet passage, brought food for the vigil, and allowed me to lean into your strength.

Thanks to those who stuck with me after Vic died, fed me, walked, called, and listened to my story with endless patience. Thank you to

Matt Hoff who manages my land and makes it possible for me to live in the place I love.

I'm grateful to Dr. Michael Eisman, our friend and family physician, who guided and loved us every step of the way. Also Dr. Jonathan Friedberg, Dr. Richard Fisher, and caring staff at Strong Memorial Hospital who did their best to treat an incurable cancer and gave Vic time to finish his work. I can't leave out Finger Lakes Coffee Roasters in the Strong Hospital lobby where I ordered decaf soy milk cappuccino for Vic many mornings. "I call this 'a why bother,'" the barista said with a grin. His simple joke got me through the day and still makes me laugh.

Thank you, Barbara Platek, for therapeutic support. You kept me from drowning in grief and helped me find a path into my new life. Thank you, Janet Wylde, for tending my grieving body with healing massage and loving kindness.

Thanks to Ellen Schmidt who welcomed the grief I poured onto pages in her writing classes and improved my writing skills. Ellen mid-wifed my creative process and saw I had a book before I did. She is my teacher and dear friend.

I'm grateful to Jill Swenson and her team at Swenson Book Development for guiding me through the process of writing and pub-lication. Jill is an excellent and empathetic editor and a writer's ally.

Thank you to others who read and commented on the first draft of the book including Tina Welling, Paul Cash, and Lynn Trudell. I'm also grateful for help from my memoir group.

I'm grateful to Larson Publications for believing in this project and embracing *Leaning into Love*. Paul Cash gave me essential editorial direction on the first draft and led me through all aspects of publishing. Amy Opperman Cash generously helped in each step of the process.

I thank my teachers Anthony Damiani, Marion Woodman, and the Dalai Lama who brought meaning and depth to my life and loss. Thank you, Naomi Shihab Nye, for teaching me much about Kindness.

I am forever grateful to Vic for helping me learn the art of love.

Endnotes

1. Juan Ramón Jiménez, "Oceans," in *The Soul Is Here for Its Own Joy*, trans. Robert Bly (New York: HarperCollins, 1995) 246.

2. Rainer Maria Rilke, "Sonnets to Orpheus: Part Two, XXVII," in *In Praise of Mortality: Selections from Rainer Maria Rilke's Duino Elegies and Sonnets to Orpheus*, trans. and ed. Anita Barrows and Joanna Macy (New York: Riverhead Books, 2005) 133. Reprinted by permission of translators.

3. Rainer Maria Rilke, "Sonnets: Part Two, XXIX," 135.

4. Rainer Maria Rilke, "Sonnets: Part One, XIII," 87.

5. Rainer Maria Rilke, "Sonnets: Part Two, XXIX," 135.

6. Rainer Maria Rilke, "Sonnets: Part One, VI," 77.

7. Rainer Maria Rilke, "Sonnets: Part Two, X," 115.

8. Emily Dickinson, #254, *The Complete Poems of Emily Dickinson*, ed. Thomas H. Johnson (Boston: Little, Brown, 1890) 116.

9. Walter Benton, "Entry April 28," *This is My Beloved* (New York: Alfred A. Knopf, 1964) 8.

10. Naomi Shihab Nye, "Kindness," *Words under the Words* (Portland, Oregon: Eight Mountain Press, 1995), 42–43.

11. Rainer Maria Rilke, "Sonnets: Part Two, I," 107.

12. Sogyal Rinpoche, *The Tibetan Book of Living and Dying*, ed. Patrick Gaffney and Andrew Harvey, (San Francisco: Harper, 1993) 316.

13. Jyoti, "Walk On," in *Graceful Passages: A Companion for Living and Dying* (Novato, CA: New World Library, 2003) 32.

14. Rainer Maria Rilke, "Pushing Through" in *Selected Poems of Rainer Maria Rilke,* trans. and ed. Robert Bly (New York: Harper and Row, 1981) 55.

15. Rainer Maria Rilke, "Tenth Duino Elegy," *The Selected Poetry of Rainer Maria Rilke,* ed. and trans. Stephen Mitchell (New York: Random House, 1982) 205.

16. Rainer Maria Rilke, "Sonnets: Part One, XII," 85.

17. Harold Arlen (music) and E.Y. Harburg (lyrics), "Over the Rainbow" in *The Wizard of Oz,* 1939.

18. Hein Stufkens and Philip Engelen, "Interview with Marie-Louise von Franz," (Küsnacht: IKON-television, November 1990, 'Passions of the Soul', part 2, IKON TV, Hilversum, Holland).